MASTERING THE CIVIL SERVICES EXAMINATION: A COMPREHENSIVE GUIDE FOR CSE ASPIRANTS

FROM PERSONAL INSIGHTS TO PROVEN STRATEGIES: CHARTING A SUCCESSFUL PATH THROUGH MY CSE JOURNEY

DR. VIJAY VARADI, PhD

THE UPSC OF INDIA: ITS HISTORICAL EVOLUTION AND IMPACT ON CONTEMPORARY INDIA

UPSC (Union Public Service Commission) of India

What is UPSC? The Union Public Service Commission (UPSC) is India's central recruiting agency. It is responsible for appointments to and examinations for All India services and group A & group B of Central services. UPSC is an autonomous constitutional body that ensures the efficient functioning of the bureaucracy in India, serving as the backbone of the administrative machinery.

Brief History:

1. **British Era**: The Royal Commission on the Superior Civil Services in India under the chairmanship of Lord Lee of Fareham was appointed in 1923, which led to the establishment of the Federal Public Service Commission (FPSC).

2. **After Independence**: After independence, the FPSC became the Union Public Service Commission on January 26, 1950, with a mandate expanded under the Constitution of India.

   Examinations conducted by UPSC: The most prominent examination conducted by UPSC is the Civil Services Examination (CSE) which recruits candidates for services such as the Indian Administrative Service (IAS), Indian Foreign Service (IFS), and Indian Police Service (IPS), among others. In addition to the CSE, UPSC conducts examinations for the Indian Forest Service, Engineering Services, Combined Medical Services, and many other central services.

How UPSC Influences Shaping Modern India:

1. **Selecting the Best**: UPSC has a rigorous examination process, ensuring that only the best and brightest candidates are inducted into the Indian bureaucracy. These officers are placed in roles across India, from remote

villages to metropolitan cities, making decisions that influence the lives of billions.

2. **Diverse Representation**: UPSC ensures representation from all parts of the country and from diverse socio-economic backgrounds. This diversity in the civil services ensures that policy-making is more holistic and representative of the needs and aspirations of all Indians.

3. **Policy Implementation**: IAS and other civil service officers play a crucial role in the implementation of government policies at the grassroots. Whether it's a new education policy, health initiative, or infrastructure project, these officers are responsible for turning the government's vision into reality.

4. **Upholding Secular and Democratic Values**: In a diverse country like India, UPSC officers play a pivotal role in upholding secular and democratic values, ensuring that every citizen's rights are protected.

5. **International Relations**: IFS officers, selected through the UPSC, represent India on the global stage, shaping the country's foreign policy and its relations with other nations.

6. **Adapting to Modern Challenges**: UPSC has been updating its examination pattern and syllabus over the years to ensure that the selected candidates are equipped to deal with modern-day challenges, be it in the realm of technology, international relations, environment, or socio-economic changes.

7. **Neutral and Impartial**: The UPSC operates autonomously and ensures that the recruitment process remains free from political or any other external influences, ensuring the bureaucracy remains neutral and functions based on the principles of the Constitution.

In conclusion, the UPSC has a monumental role in shaping the future of India. By selecting competent individuals into the civil services, it ensures that the country's administrative machinery functions effectively, and policies are implemented for the betterment of the nation.

THE SIGNIFICANCE OF UPSC IN INDIA: REASONS FOR ITS PIVOTAL ROLE

The UPSC (Union Public Service Commission) plays an integral role in the governance and administration of India. Its importance stems from various functions and responsibilities vested in it by the Constitution of India. Here's how and why the UPSC plays a vital role in the country:

1. **Gatekeeper to Civil Services:**
   - **How:** The UPSC conducts various examinations, with the Civil Services Examination (CSE) being the most prominent. Through these examinations, the UPSC selects candidates for various administrative positions, including the Indian Administrative Service (IAS), Indian Police Service (IPS), and Indian Foreign Service (IFS), among others.
   - **Why:** These services form the backbone of the Indian administrative machinery. IAS officers, for instance, serve at key positions in the central and state bureaucracies, making them instrumental in policy formulation, implementation, and public administration at large.

2. **Ensuring Meritocracy:**
   - **How:** UPSC examinations are rigorous and highly competitive. They are designed to test a candidate's analytical abilities, general knowledge, decision-making skills, and more.
   - **Why:** This ensures that only the most competent individuals enter the civil services, thereby maintaining the integrity and efficiency of India's bureaucracy.

3. **Upholding Constitutional Values:**
   - **How:** The UPSC operates autonomously, free from any external pressures or influences. This independence ensures that recruitments are made impartially.

- ◆ **Why:** An unbiased recruitment process ensures that the civil service remains secular, neutral, and works in the spirit of the Constitution, thus preserving the democratic ethos of the country.

4. **Representation and Diversity:**

   - ◆ **How:** UPSC examinations are open to all eligible Indian citizens, ensuring candidates from diverse geographical, social, and economic backgrounds have a fair shot at entering the services.

   - ◆ **Why:** Such diversity ensures that India's bureaucracy is representative of its population, leading to more inclusive and sensitive policy-making and administration.

5. **Continuous Adaptation:**

   - ◆ **How:** UPSC periodically revises the examination pattern, syllabus, and recruitment processes to align with the changing socio-economic and technological landscape of the country.

   - ◆ **Why:** This ensures that the civil services are equipped to handle modern challenges, be it in technology, environment, economics, or governance.

6. **Professional Development:**

   - ◆ **How:** Apart from initial recruitment, UPSC also plays a role in the promotion and placement of officers at various stages of their careers.

   - ◆ **Why:** This ensures that officers with the right skill sets and experience are placed in positions where they can be most effective.

7. **Checks and Balances:**

   - ◆ **How:** UPSC also handles disciplinary cases against civil servants. It can advise the government on any matter related to personnel administration.

   - ◆ **Why:** This keeps the civil services accountable and ensures that any misconduct or inefficiency can be appropriately addressed.

In essence, the UPSC's role is not just limited to recruitment but extends to maintaining the ethos, efficiency, and integrity of India's civil services. By doing so, it plays a pivotal role in ensuring effective governance, policy implementation, and upholding the democratic values enshrined in the Constitution.

COLLABORATIVE LEARNING FOR CIVIL SERVICE EXAMINATION PREPARATION: STRATEGIES AND AUTHENTICITIES

Preparing for civil service examinations is a demanding and multifaceted journey that requires dedication, strategy, and effective learning methods. One of the most impactful approaches to achieving success in these exams is through collaborative learning. This method leverages the collective effort and shared vision of a group to enhance individual and group performance. This article explores the strategies and authenticity of collaborative learning in the context of civil service examination preparation.

The Power of Collaborative Learning

Collaborative learning involves students working together in small groups to achieve common academic goals. This approach is particularly beneficial for civil service exam preparation due to the following reasons:

1. **Shared Resources:** When a group of aspirants collaborates, they can pool their resources, such as books, notes, and online materials. This reduces the individual burden of acquiring all the necessary resources.

2. **Diverse Perspectives:** Each member of the group brings their unique perspective and understanding of topics. This diversity can lead to a more comprehensive grasp of complex subjects.

3. **Motivation and Support:** Preparing for civil service exams can be isolating and stressful. Collaborative learning provides a support system where members can motivate and encourage each other, making the journey less daunting.

4. **Accountability:** Being part of a group creates a sense of accountability. Members are more likely to stay committed to their study schedules and goals when they know others are relying on them.

Implementing Collaborative Learning: Strategies

To effectively implement collaborative learning in civil service exam preparation, consider the following strategies:

1. **Forming Study Groups:** Assemble a group of like-minded individuals who share the same vision and mission. The group should ideally consist of 4-6 members to maintain focus and manageability.

2. **Structured Meetings:** Schedule regular meetings, either daily or weekly, to discuss progress, share insights, and tackle difficult topics. Ensure that each meeting has a clear agenda and objectives.

3. **Role Assignment:** Assign specific roles to each member, such as note-taker, discussion leader, or timekeeper. This ensures that meetings are organized and productive.

4. **Resource Sharing:** Create a shared repository for study materials, such as cloud storage or a collaborative document. Members can upload notes, practice questions, and useful links for everyone's benefit.

5. **Peer Teaching:** Encourage members to take turns explaining topics to the group. Teaching is a powerful way to reinforce one's own understanding and helps clarify doubts for others.

6. **Mock Tests and Discussions:** Regularly conduct mock tests and group discussions. Analyze performance and discuss mistakes to identify areas for improvement.

7. **Flexibility and Adaptability:** Be open to adjusting study plans based on the group's progress and individual needs. Flexibility is key to maintaining a healthy and productive study environment.

Authenticity in Collaborative Learning

Authenticity in collaborative learning is crucial for it to be effective. Here are ways to ensure that the collaboration remains genuine and beneficial:

1. **Honest Communication:** Foster an environment where members feel comfortable sharing their thoughts, doubts, and weaknesses without fear of judgment.

2. **Constructive Feedback:** Provide and accept feedback in a constructive manner. Focus on solutions and improvements rather than criticism.

3. **Respect and Inclusivity:** Respect each member's contributions and ensure that everyone's voice is heard. Inclusivity strengthens the group's cohesion and effectiveness.

4. **Commitment to Shared Goals:** Align individual goals with the group's objectives. Ensure that every member is committed to the group's success as much as their own.

5. **Transparency:** Maintain transparency in resource sharing, role assignments, and progress tracking. This builds trust and enhances collaborative efforts.

Conclusion

Collaborative learning is a powerful method for preparing for civil service examinations. By forming study groups, sharing resources, and maintaining authenticity in interactions, aspirants can enhance their learning experience and increase their chances of success. The journey of preparing for civil service exams is challenging, but with the support and collective effort of a dedicated group, it becomes a more achievable and rewarding endeavor. Embrace collaborative learning and witness the transformation of individual aspirations into collective triumphs.

THE UPSC AND THE INDIAN CONSTITUTION: ORIGINS, ESTABLISHMENT AS A CONSTITUTIONAL ENTITY, AND ALIGNMENT WITH INDIA'S CONSTITUTIONAL PRINCIPLES

The Union Public Service Commission (UPSC) is rooted in the Constitution of India. The provisions related to its formation, functions, and powers are enshrined in the Constitution, making it a constitutional agency. Let's delve deeper into its constitutional role and how it aligns with the larger ethos of the Constitution of India.

1. **Constitutional Role in Setting up UPSC:** The UPSC finds its origins in Articles 315 to 323 in Part XIV of the Constitution. Some key provisions are:

    ◆ **Article 315:** Establishes the UPSC to conduct examinations for recruitment to all India services and higher central services.

    ◆ **Article 316:** Deals with the appointment and term of service of the members of the UPSC.

    ◆ **Article 317:** Speaks about the removal of a member from the UPSC.

    ◆ **Article 320:** Lays out the functions of the UPSC, including conducting examinations, assisting states on request, and advising the President on disciplinary matters.

2. **How it became a Constitutional Agency:** When the Constitution of India was adopted on January 26, 1950, it provided for the establishment of the UPSC, making it a constitutional body. Before the Constitution, there existed the Federal Public Service Commission under the Government of India Act, 1935. With the commencement of the Constitution, this body was transformed into the UPSC.

3. **How UPSC aligns with the Constitution of India:**

♦ **Upholding Meritocracy and Equality:** By conducting impartial and rigorous examinations, the UPSC ensures merit-based selection, upholding the principles of equality and justice. This is in tune with the constitutional mandate of ensuring equal opportunities for all citizens.

♦ **Representation:** The UPSC follows the reservation guidelines as prescribed by the Constitution to provide representation to Scheduled Castes, Scheduled Tribes, and Other Backward Classes, ensuring an inclusive administrative framework.

♦ **Neutrality and Impartiality:** Being a constitutional body, the UPSC functions autonomously, free from any executive or political influence. This ensures that the selection process remains neutral and independent, producing a bureaucracy that can serve without prejudice and uphold the secular and democratic ideals of the Constitution.

♦ **Advisory Role:** The UPSC, under Article 320, has an advisory role. It can advise the President on matters related to personnel administration. This role ensures that the executive's decisions align with the constitutional values and principles.

♦ **Decentralization:** The Constitution, recognizing the diversity and vastness of India, allows state governments to seek the UPSC's assistance in selecting personnel for state services. This cooperative federalism ensures a standardized and high-quality administrative setup across the country.

♦ **Disciplinary Role:** The UPSC plays a role in ensuring accountability within the services. By advising the President on disciplinary matters, it upholds the integrity and ethics of the bureaucracy, which is vital for a constitutional democracy.

In summary, the UPSC, as a constitutional body, plays a pivotal role in ensuring that the administrative framework of India is built on the foundational principles of the Constitution. It ensures a meritocratic, representative, and accountable civil service that can effectively serve the diverse and complex needs of the Indian polity while upholding constitutional values.

THE SYMBIOTIC RELATIONSHIP BETWEEN UPSC AND CAT: WORKING IN TANDEM FOR IMPROVED INTEGRITY AND DECISION-MAKING

The Union Public Service Commission (UPSC) and the Central Administrative Tribunal (CAT) are both integral components of the Indian administrative structure, but they have distinct functions and roles. However, they do intersect in certain matters, mainly related to disputes and grievances of civil servants.

UPSC:

- **Role:** The primary role of the UPSC is recruitment. It conducts examinations and selects candidates for various All India Services, Central Services, and other related administrative positions.

- **Functions:** Apart from recruitment, UPSC also advises the President of India on disciplinary matters concerning civil servants.

CAT:

- **Establishment:** The Central Administrative Tribunal was established by an Act of Parliament in 1985, namely the Administrative Tribunals Act, 1985.

- **Role:** CAT's primary role is to adjudicate disputes and complaints related to the recruitment and service conditions of persons appointed to public services and posts concerning the Union or other authorities under the control of the Government of India. This includes grievances related to seniority, promotions, transfers, disciplinary actions, and other matters related to employment conditions.

Link between UPSC and CAT:

1. **Recruitment Disputes:** If there are grievances or disputes related to the recruitment process conducted by the UPSC, the affected parties can approach CAT for redressal.

2. **Disciplinary Actions:** The UPSC advises the President of India on disciplinary matters. If a civil servant is aggrieved by a disciplinary action that's been recommended or advised upon by the UPSC, they can challenge it before the CAT.

Integrity and Better Decision-making:

1. **Checks and Balances:** The existence of CAT ensures there's a system of checks and balances in place. If the UPSC or any other recruitment body makes an error or acts in a manner that's perceived as unfair, CAT serves as a platform where such decisions can be reviewed and rectified.

2. **Impartial Adjudication:** CAT functions as an independent body, ensuring that grievances related to public services are addressed impartially, reinforcing trust in the system.

3. **Specialized Knowledge:** CAT, being a specialized tribunal, has a better understanding of service matters and can adjudicate complex service-related issues more efficiently than regular courts.

4. **Quick Resolution:** One of the intentions behind setting up CAT was to provide speedy relief to civil servants, ensuring that service-related grievances don't linger in the judiciary for extended periods.

In essence, while the UPSC focuses on recruitment and advising on disciplinary matters, CAT ensures that any disputes or grievances arising out of these processes are addressed fairly and efficiently. The existence of CAT enhances the integrity of the administrative system and ensures better decision-making by providing an avenue for redressal and review.

THE RECRUITMENT PROCESS FOR CIVIL SERVANTS THROUGH UPSC

The Union Public Service Commission (UPSC) conducts the Civil Services Examination (CSE) to select candidates for various Civil Services of the Government of India, including the Indian Administrative Service (IAS), Indian Foreign Service (IFS), and Indian Police Service (IPS), among others. The selection procedure is known for its rigor and is divided into three main stages:

1. **Preliminary Examination (Prelims):**
   - **Nature:** Objective type (Multiple Choice Questions).
   - **Papers:** Two papers.
   - **General Studies Paper I:** Tests on current events, history of India, Indian national movement, Indian and world geography, Indian polity and governance, economic and social development, environmental ecology, general science.
   - **General Studies Paper II (CSAT - Civil Services Aptitude Test):** Comprehension, interpersonal skills, logical reasoning and analytical ability, decision-making and problem-solving, general mental ability, basic numeracy, data interpretation.
   - **Purpose:** It's a screening test. Marks secured in this stage are not counted for final ranking but are essential for qualification to the Mains Examination.

2. **Main Examination (Mains):**
   - **Nature:** Descriptive type (Essay writing and answer writing).
   - **Papers:** Nine papers in total.
   - **Qualifying Papers:** Two papers of language proficiency – One in any Indian language and another in English. These are qualifying in nature, and the marks obtained aren't counted for the final ranking.

◆ **Papers to be Counted for Merit:** Seven papers, including:

◆ Essay

◆ General Studies I (Indian Heritage and Culture, History, and Geography of the World and Society)

◆ General Studies II (Governance, Constitution, Polity, Social Justice, and International relations)

◆ General Studies III (Technology, Economic Development, Biodiversity, Environment, Security, and Disaster Management)

◆ General Studies IV (Ethics, Integrity, and Aptitude)

◆ Optional Subject - Paper I

◆ Optional Subject - Paper II

◆ **Purpose:** Marks obtained in the Main Examination are counted for qualification to the Interview and also for the final ranking.

3. Personality Test (Interview):

◆ **Nature:** It's not a test of specialized knowledge but rather assesses the overall personality, attitude, and aptitude of the candidate. It evaluates the candidate's mental caliber, critical powers of assimilation, balance of judgment, and leadership skills, among other qualities.

◆ **Marks:** The interview carries 275 marks.

◆ **Purpose:** Marks obtained in the interview are added to the marks obtained in the Mains to produce the final rank of the candidate.

After the interview, a final list of selected candidates is prepared based on the combined marks from the Mains Examination and the Interview. Depending on their rankings and service preferences, candidates are then allotted various services.

The entire selection procedure of the UPSC Civil Services Examination is one of the most exhaustive and challenging competitive exams in India, designed to select the best talent for administrative roles in the country.

ANNUAL AVERAGE OF VACANCIES FILLED IN INDIA: AN OVERVIEW

The number of posts filled through the UPSC Civil Services Examination (CSE) varies each year based on the requirements projected by various departments and services of the Government of India.

On average, over the past few years leading up to my last update in September 2021, the number of vacancies announced annually for the CSE has ranged from around 700 to 1,200 posts. This includes vacancies for prestigious services like the Indian Administrative Service (IAS), Indian Police Service (IPS), Indian Foreign Service (IFS), and various other Central Services.

However, the actual number of vacancies can fluctuate based on factors such as:

- Retirements in the bureaucracy.

- Expansion or creation of new departments or services.

- Policy decisions regarding staffing and recruitment.

- Any additional requirements that may arise in a particular year.

It's also worth noting that the UPSC CSE is just one of many recruitment processes managed by the UPSC. Other examinations, like the Engineering Services Examination, Combined Defence Services Examination, and more, also lead to recruitment in various departments and services. Each of these has its own set of vacancies.

For the most accurate and current figures for any particular year, it's best to refer to the official notification released by the UPSC for the Civil Services Examination of that year.

WHAT IS THE SUCCESS RATE OF THIS EXAM AND ASPIRANTS?

The UPSC Civil Services Examination (CSE) is one of the most challenging competitive exams in India, and its success rate is relatively low compared to the number of aspirants.

To understand the success rate, let's break down the numbers (based on data up to September 2021):

1. **Number of Aspirants:** Every year, approximately 8 to 10 lakh candidates apply for the UPSC CSE. However, not all of them appear for the Preliminary examination. The actual number of candidates taking the Prelims usually hovers around 4 to 6 lakh.

2. **Preliminary Examination:** Out of the candidates who appear for the Prelims, typically about 10,000 to 15,000 candidates (or even fewer some years) qualify for the Mains examination. This translates to a success rate of about 2-3% for the Prelims stage.

3. **Main Examination:** Out of the candidates who appear for the Mains examination, generally around 2,000 to 3,000 candidates are selected for the Personality Test (Interview). This means a success rate of roughly 15-20% for the Mains stage.

4. **Final Selection:** Finally, based on the vacancies for that particular year (which can range from around 700 to 1,200 as mentioned earlier), candidates are selected after the Interview. So, from the original number of Prelims candidates, less than 0.5% get recommended for various civil services.

In essence, the overall success rate, considering the entire process from Prelims to the Interview, is well below 1% of the total number of candidates who appear for the Preliminary examination.

The low success rate underscores the rigorous nature of the examination and the high standards set by the UPSC for the selection of candidates into the prestigious civil services of India. This also explains why many aspirants attempt the examination multiple times to secure a good rank or even just to clear the various stages.

SECURING A SPOT IN THE ELITE 0.5%: KEY TRAITS FOR UPSC ASPIRANTS TO ACHIEVE SUCCESS

Cracking the UPSC Civil Services Examination (CSE) and being among the top 0.5% requires a combination of rigorous preparation, the right strategies, and certain innate qualities. While each successful candidate has their own journey and approach, some common traits and strategies can be identified among toppers:

1. **Consistent and Systematic Preparation:** This is not an exam one can crack with sporadic bouts of intensive study. Consistency over months and even years is key.

2. **Comprehensive Understanding:** The UPSC values depth of understanding. It's essential to grasp the underlying principles and concepts, rather than just memorizing facts.

3. **Current Affairs Acumen:** Given the dynamic nature of the exam, staying updated with current affairs is crucial. Regularly reading standard newspapers and following reliable current affairs magazines helps.

4. **Practice:** Regularly writing mock tests and answer writing practice for Mains can make a significant difference. This improves time management, answer structuring, and the ability to recall relevant information under exam conditions.

5. **Analytical Skills:** UPSC questions often require analytical skills, especially in the Mains and Interview. Developing the ability to critically analyze issues is essential.

6. **Perseverance:** Due to the vast syllabus and the competitive nature of the CSE, perseverance is crucial. Many successful candidates clear the exam after multiple attempts.

7. **Effective Time Management:** Efficiently managing one's time during preparation and the examination (especially in Prelims and Mains) is crucial.

8. **Holistic Development:** UPSC is not just about academic brilliance. It seeks candidates with a well-rounded personality, good decision-making skills, empathy, and integrity, especially evident in the Interview stage.

9. **Physical and Mental Well-being:** Regular physical activity and mindfulness practices can help manage the stress and pressure of the examination process.

10. **Learning from Mistakes:** Regularly reviewing one's performance in mock tests, understanding mistakes, and learning from them is vital.

11. **Guidance:** While many candidates clear the exam through self-study, having a mentor or joining a coaching institute (only if required) can provide direction. However, it's crucial to rely on one's judgment and avoid being overwhelmed by the multitude of resources available.

12. **Focused Approach:** While the syllabus is vast, it's crucial to prioritize topics based on their importance and one's strengths and weaknesses.

13. **Adaptability:** The nature of the UPSC exam can be unpredictable, with changing patterns and types of questions. Aspirants must be adaptable to these changes and be prepared to modify their strategies if necessary.

14. **Curiosity:** A genuine interest in understanding the world, its systems, and its history can make the preparation journey less tedious and more enriching. Curiosity can help retain information better.

15. **Discipline:** Setting a daily routine and sticking to it, avoiding distractions, and ensuring that daily targets are met are all signs of discipline—an essential trait for any UPSC aspirant.

16. **Self-awareness:** Recognizing one's strengths and weaknesses allows for targeted preparation. It's important to work on areas of improvement while also leveraging strengths.

17. **Effective Note-making:** The ability to sift through vast amounts of information and condense it into concise, easy-to-revise notes can be a game-changer during revision.

18. **Interpersonal Skills:** These are particularly essential for the interview stage, where interaction with the board members tests a candidate's ability to communicate effectively and present their ideas clearly.

19. **Empathy:** Understanding and respecting diverse perspectives is essential, especially for a civil servant. Demonstrating empathy in answers can also fetch better marks.

20. **Optimism:** There will be days of doubt, fatigue, and low motivation. Maintaining a positive outlook and believing in the process and oneself can make the journey smoother.

21. **Patience:** Given that many aspirants take multiple attempts to clear the exam, patience is a virtue. It's essential to understand that the preparation itself is a valuable experience, teaching life skills and imparting knowledge.

22. **Critical Thinking:** Beyond rote learning, UPSC values candidates who can think critically, present multiple perspectives, and provide solutions to problems.

23. **Resource Management:** With a plethora of study materials available, aspirants should be judicious in selecting the right resources to avoid information overload. It's often more effective to revise a single source multiple times than to jump between multiple sources.

24. **Networking:** Engaging with fellow aspirants can offer fresh perspectives, share resources, and even provide moral support. Study groups, if utilized correctly, can be beneficial.

25. **Continuous Learning Attitude:** Instead of viewing the UPSC journey as a means to an end, viewing it as an opportunity for continuous learning can be mentally rewarding and less stressful.

Remember, while these traits and strategies are commonly found in successful candidates, the UPSC journey is deeply personal. Each aspirant must find what works best for them, stay true to their strengths, and continually adapt and learn. The journey requires resilience, a deep-seated commitment, and an unwavering belief in oneself.

Lastly, while these traits are helpful, each aspirant is unique. It's essential to find one's rhythm, trust the process, and maintain a balance between preparation and personal well-being.

INSIGHTS FROM SUCCESSFUL CANDIDATES: TOP BOOK RECOMMENDATIONS, TOOLS, AND TECHNIQUES FOR UPSC PREPARATION

Many successful UPSC Civil Services Examination (CSE) aspirants share their strategies, booklists, and suggestions after their achievements. While individual strategies vary, some commonly suggested resources and techniques include:

Books:

1. **History:**
   - *Ancient and Medieval India:* Books by R.S. Sharma and Satish Chandra.
   - *Modern India:* 'India's Struggle for Independence' by Bipan Chandra.
   - *World History:* 'Norman Lowe' or Arjun Dev.

2. **Geography:**
   - NCERT books (Class 6-12).
   - 'Certificate Physical and Human Geography' by Goh Cheng Leong.

3. **Polity:**
   - 'Indian Polity' by M. Laxmikanth.

4. **Economics:**
   - NCERT books.
   - 'Indian Economy' by Ramesh Singh.

5. **Environment:**
   - 'Environment' by Shankar IAS Academy.
   - NCERT books.

6. **General Science:**
   - NCERT books (Class 6-10).

7. Art and Culture:

- 'Indian Art and Culture' by Nitin Singhania.

8. Ethics:

- 'Ethics, Integrity, and Aptitude' by Subba Rao and P.N. Roy Chowdhury.

9. Current Affairs:

- Newspapers like 'The Hindu' or 'Indian Express'.

- Monthly magazines like 'Yojana', 'Kurukshetra', and compilations by coaching institutes.

Tools & Techniques:

1. **Revision:** Multiple revisions are critical. Most toppers stress the importance of revising the study material 3-4 times, if not more.

2. **Answer Writing:** Practice answer writing regularly. Enrolling in test series or practicing previous years' question papers can be beneficial.

3. **Notes Making:** Making concise notes, especially for current affairs and important topics, helps during revision.

4. **Mind Maps:** Visual tools like mind maps can assist in organizing information and improving retention.

5. **Newspaper Reading:** Regularly reading a standard newspaper helps in essay paper, ethics case studies, and interview preparation.

6. **Online Resources:** Websites like PRS India, PIB (Press Information Bureau), and IDSA can provide deeper insights into various topics.

7. **Group Study:** It can be beneficial for discussions and understanding diverse perspectives, but it's essential to choose study partners wisely.

8. **Mock Tests:** Taking regular mock tests helps in gauging preparation levels and improving time management.

9. **Stay Updated with UPSC Syllabus:** Always align your preparation with the official UPSC syllabus. It acts as a checklist to ensure that no topic is left out.

10. **Focused Preparation:** Instead of gathering countless resources, stick to a few standard books and revise them multiple times.

General Suggestions:

1. **Health:** Take care of physical and mental health. Regular exercise, meditation, or any other relaxation techniques can help manage stress.

2. **Stay Positive:** Believe in yourself and your preparation. Avoid negative influences and stay motivated.

3. **Balance:** While studying is important, take regular breaks, engage in hobbies, and ensure that there's a balance.

4. **Continuous Learning:** Treat every day as a learning opportunity. Every topic you read adds value, irrespective of the outcome in the exam.

Certainly! The UPSC journey is nuanced, and there are several other dimensions to consider. Here are some additional insights, tips, and suggestions:

Digital Platforms & Apps:

1. **YouTube Channels:** There are numerous channels that provide lectures on specific topics, discussions, and strategy videos. Vision IAS, Drishti IAS, and Unacademy are some popular options.

2. **Mobile Apps:** Apps like 'The Hindu', 'PIB', 'UPSC Pathshala', and 'Civilsdaily' can be useful for current affairs and daily quiz practice.

Books and Reports:

1. **Government Reports:** Economic Survey, India Yearbook, and reports from NITI Aayog provide data and government perspectives on various issues.

2. **ARC (Administrative Reforms Commission) Reports:** These are especially important for the Public Administration optional and topics related to governance.

Interview Preparation:

1. **Diverse Reading:** Apart from newspapers, reading magazines, journals, or even novels can offer a broader perspective, enriching answers and discussions during the interview.

2. **Mock Interviews:** Enroll in mock interview sessions. They can provide insights into body language, content, and presentation.

3. **Self-awareness:** Be ready to answer questions related to your personal background, hobbies, home state, and graduation subjects.

Additional Tips:

1. **Avoid Multitasking:** Focus on one subject or topic at a time to ensure depth and clarity.

2. **Interlink Subjects:** Try to connect concepts from different subjects. For instance, linking economic policies with their historical background or their geographical implications.

3. **Past Papers:** Regularly solve previous year question papers. It helps understand the pattern, types of questions, and areas of importance.

4. **Avoid Last-minute Inclusions:** Don't pick up new books or materials just before the exam. It can lead to confusion and stress.

5. **Updates on Exam Pattern:** Stay updated with any changes in the UPSC pattern or syllabus.

6. **Feedback Loop:** After mock tests, seek feedback, introspect, and work on areas of improvement.

7. **Stay Connected:** Engage with fellow aspirants through online forums like Quora, Telegram groups, or UPSC-specific platforms. Share resources, clarify doubts, and discuss topics.

8. **Rest and Sleep:** Ensure you get adequate sleep, especially as the exam approaches. A well-rested mind is more alert and efficient.

9. **Mental Resilience:** Stay mentally strong. There will be highs and lows in the preparation journey. How you manage them determines a significant part of your success.

10. **Optional Subject:** Choose your optional subject wisely. Consider your interest in the subject, availability of resources, and scoring trends.

Detailed Study Plan:

1. **Long-Term & Short-Term Goals:** Break down the vast syllabus into monthly, weekly, and daily targets. This makes the preparation more structured and manageable.

2. **Time Allocation:** Dedicate specific time slots for different subjects. For example, you might allocate mornings for static subjects like history or geography and evenings for dynamic subjects like current affairs.

Optional Subject Strategy:

1. **Deep Dive:** Once you've chosen your optional, immerse yourself completely. It often makes the difference in your overall ranking.

2. **Previous Year Questions:** Analyze past papers of your optional subject to understand the trend and depth required.

3. **Standard Books for Optional:** Different optional subjects have specific reference books. For instance, for Sociology, many prefer 'Sociology: Themes and Perspectives' by Haralambos and Holborn.

Resource Management:

1. **Limit Resources:** For every subject, limit yourself to 1-2 primary books. Avoid the temptation to gather too many materials.

2. **Digital vs. Print:** While digital resources (websites, apps, PDFs) are vast and easily accessible, some find printed material better for retention. Find what works best for you.

Enhancing Answer Writing:

1. **Introduction and Conclusion:** Begin your answers with a clear introduction and end with a relevant conclusion. This structure fetches better marks.

2. **Diagrams and Flowcharts:** Incorporate these in your answers, especially in subjects like Geography and Science, to make your answers more appealing.

3. **Use Current Affairs:** Supplement your answers with recent examples or data from current affairs to make them more relevant.

Self-Care and Stress Management:

1. **Meditation and Breathing Exercises:** These can help reduce anxiety, especially as the exam day approaches.

2. **Hobbies:** Regularly engage in hobbies or activities you love. It acts as a stress buster.

3. **Diet:** A balanced diet plays an integral role in maintaining energy and focus. Stay hydrated and include brain-boosting foods like nuts, seeds, and fruits.

Staying Updated:

1. **Government Websites:** Regularly visit official websites such as the Ministry of External Affairs, Ministry of Environment, Forest and Climate Change, etc., for official statements, data, and policies.

2. **Annual Reports:** These offer a comprehensive overview of a ministry's work throughout the year and can be valuable for both prelims and mains.

3. **Seminars and Webinars:** Attend seminars or webinars related to IAS preparation. It offers fresh perspectives and insights.

Avoiding Common Mistakes:

1. **Isolation:** While solitude is often required, complete isolation can lead to burnout. Regular interactions can offer breaks and fresh perspectives.

2. **Overconfidence or Underconfidence:** Both can be detrimental. Regularly evaluate your preparation to maintain a balanced perspective.

3. **Neglecting Prelims or Mains:** Some aspirants focus too much on one at the expense of the other. Both stages require dedicated and specific preparation.

Final Thoughts:

Preparation for UPSC is a marathon, not a sprint. It requires endurance, patience, and adaptability. Given the vastness of the syllabus and the unpredictability of questions, aspirants should focus on building a strong foundational knowledge while also developing the ability to think critically and analytically.

Every aspirant's journey is unique. While these guidelines provide a general roadmap, it's crucial for each individual to reflect on their strengths and weaknesses, adapt strategies accordingly, and most importantly, enjoy the learning process.

While these are general suggestions and resources based on feedback from several successful candidates, it's essential for every aspirant to understand what works best for them and customize their preparation accordingly.

Remember, while these tips come from a collection of advice from successful candidates, it's crucial for aspirants to tailor their strategies based on their strengths, weaknesses, and unique circumstances. Success in UPSC often comes from a blend of smart work, hard work, persistence, and self-belief.

THE ROLE OF INTERPERSONAL SKILLS, INTERDISCIPLINARY LEARNING, AND COLLABORATIVE STUDY METHODS IN ENHANCING PREPARATION

Absolutely! The UPSC Civil Services Examination isn't just about rote memorization. It is designed to assess the all-around intellectual traits and depth of understanding of the candidates. Let's delve into the mentioned skills and mechanisms:

1. **Interpersonal Skills:**

   1. **Interview Phase:** UPSC interviews aren't just a test of knowledge but also of personality. Interpersonal skills such as active listening, effective communication, empathy, and the ability to handle disagreements diplomatically are essential.

   2. **On the Job:** Once selected, civil servants often work in teams, lead departments, and interact with the public. Effective interpersonal skills are vital for collaboration, negotiation, and conflict resolution.

2. **Cross-Subject Learnings:**

   1. **Holistic Understanding:** UPSC syllabus is inter-disciplinary. For instance, understanding the socio-economic implications of a historical event or the geographical context of a political issue can enrich answers.

   2. **Answer Enrichment:** In mains, you can quote relevant facts from different subjects to support your answers. For instance, in an essay about climate change, integrating data from geography, economics, and even international relations can make your essay stand out.

3. Combined Learning (Share and Learn) Mechanism:

1. **Group Discussions:** Discussing complex topics with peers can offer multiple perspectives, enhancing depth and clarity.

2. **Doubt Resolution:** It's easier to get your doubts clarified by discussing them with fellow aspirants.

3. **Mock Tests & Feedback:** Peer review of answers can offer constructive feedback. Sometimes, a fellow aspirant might provide an insight that you hadn't considered.

4. **Staying Motivated:** UPSC preparation can be a long, sometimes lonely journey. Being in a study group can offer moral support and keep spirits high.

5. **Sharing Resources:** Every aspirant might have access to different study materials and resources. Sharing them can benefit everyone in the group.

4. Time Management:

1. **Pomodoro Technique:** Use a timer to break down work into intervals, traditionally 25 minutes in length, separated by short breaks. It keeps you focused and ensures regular rest to the brain.

2. **Task Prioritization:** Focus on high-yield topics and areas of personal weakness first.

5. Active Learning:

1. **Teaching:** One of the best ways to ensure you understand a topic is to teach it to someone else. Explaining complex topics can help cement your understanding.

2. **Flashcards:** Using tools like Anki or Quizlet to make digital flashcards can assist in quick revisions and better retention.

6. Critical Thinking and Application:

1. **Case Studies:** Use real-world case studies to understand and apply theoretical concepts. It aids in the development of analytical skills.

2. **Debates:** Engaging in or observing debates on relevant topics can help develop a balanced viewpoint and improve critical thinking.

7. Reg6ular Health and Fitness Routine:

1. **Physical Exercise:** Regular physical activity, be it jogging, yoga, or any sport, can help improve mental clarity and reduce stress.

2. **Meditation and Mindfulness:** Techniques like deep breathing, meditation, or even short periods of silence can help improve concentration and keep anxiety at bay.

8. Use of Technology:

1. **Educational Platforms:** Websites like Coursera, Udemy, or Khan Academy offer courses on a plethora of topics which can aid in understanding complex subjects.

2. **Podcasts:** There are numerous podcasts on current affairs, history, and more which can be listened to during commutes or breaks.

9. Self-assessments:

1. **SWOT Analysis:** Regularly conduct a SWOT (Strengths, Weaknesses, Opportunities, Threats) analysis of your preparation to fine-tune your strategy.

2. **Regular Mock Testing:** Not just for practice but also to understand the patterns of mistakes you're making.

10. Environment:

1. Study Space: Maintain a clean, organized, and dedicated study space. An environment conducive to studying can boost productivity.

2. Limit Distractions: Tools like "Cold Turkey" or "Forest" can block distracting websites or apps.

11. Diverse Reading:

1. **Non-fiction Books:** Books related to behavioral economics, psychology, sociology, etc., can offer unique perspectives and examples to quote in essays and answers.

2. **Autobiographies:** These can provide insights into leadership, ethics, and governance.

12. Networking:

1. **Mentorship:** If possible, seek mentorship from previous year's toppers or experienced teachers. Their insights and feedback can be invaluable.

2. **Online Forums:** Platforms like ForumIAS, UPSC Pathshala, etc., can be useful for resource sharing, doubt clearing, and discussions.

13. Visualization and Positive Affirmations:

14. Visualize your success. This mental exercise can be a source of motivation.

15. Use positive affirmations to build confidence and combat negative thoughts.

16. Mind Mapping:

1. **Tools:** Use applications like XMind or MindMeister to create mind maps. They help organize information hierarchically and visualize connections between concepts.

17. Note-Taking Tools:

1. **Evernote:** It allows you to clip web pages, create checklists, and sync notes across devices.

2. **OneNote:** A Microsoft tool suitable for organizing notes in a notebook-like format with sections and pages.

18. Revision Techniques:

1. **Spaced Repetition:** Using apps like Anki, you can use this technique to revise what you've learned at increasing intervals, thereby improving memory retention.

2. **Cornell Notes System:** A systematic format for condensing and organizing notes.

19. Current Affairs Digestion:

1. **Feedly:** An RSS feed aggregator where you can follow multiple news websites, blogs, or portals to get your daily dose of news and articles.

2. **Pocket:** Allows you to save articles, videos, or web pages to view later, helping you curate content for revision.

20. Time Tracking & Productivity:

1. **Toggl:** Track how much time you spend on various subjects or topics.

2. **Focus@Will:** A platform providing background music based on neuroscience to improve concentration.

21. Discussion & Peer Interaction:

1. **Telegram & Discord:** There are several UPSC dedicated groups and channels where aspirants share resources, discuss topics, and conduct quizzes.

22. Practice Questions & Mock Tests:

1. **Insights on India & IAS baba:** They offer daily current affairs quizzes, answer writing challenges, and more.

23. Interactive Learning:

1. **Kahoot:** While traditionally used in classroom settings, it can be employed in study groups to create quiz competitions, enhancing retention through interactive learning.

24. Digital Study Aids:

1. **Quizlet:** An online tool to create flashcards, quizzes, and games.

2. **Grammarly:** To improve your English writing skills, essential for mains and essay papers.

25. Podcasting & Audiobooks:

26. **Audible:** Listen to non-fiction books that broaden your horizons and understanding of various subjects.

27. **Google Podcasts:** Follow relevant channels that discuss current events, public policy, history, etc.

28. Language Learning (for Indian languages):

29. **Duolingo:** If you opt for a regional language as your optional or for the language paper, Duolingo can help you get a grasp of the basics.

30. Simulated Exam Environment:

31. Set aside days where you replicate the actual exam scenario. This will help in acclimatizing to the pressure of the real exam.

32. Goal Setting & Tracking:

33. **Trello:** A versatile tool where you can set goals, create task lists, and track your progress. It's especially handy for visual learners.

34. Relaxation & Breaks:

35. **Calm or Headspace:** Meditation apps that can help you take short breaks, reduce stress, and improve mindfulness.

36. **Multisensory Learning:** Blend various learning modes – visual (diagrams, infographics), auditory (podcasts, audiobooks), and kinesthetic (writing, interactive quizzes) to enhance retention.

While all these tools and techniques can be immensely beneficial, it's essential to remember not to get overwhelmed. Pick tools that resonate with your learning style, and don't spread yourself too thin by trying to utilize everything at once. The primary focus should always remain on the core content and consistent practice.

Remember, while these methods are beneficial, it's crucial to ensure they align with one's individual learning style and personal circumstances. Each aspirant's journey is unique, and the key is to remain adaptable and resilient.

These skills and mechanisms not only assist in cracking the UPSC examination but also prove invaluable once the aspirant becomes a civil servant. The real-world scenarios demand a lot more than mere bookish knowledge. Effective communication, collaboration, holistic understanding, and the ability to approach problems from various angles are crucial for a civil servant's role.

Certainly! Beyond the traditional methods and the ones previously mentioned, there are numerous other tools and techniques that aspirants can employ to boost their UPSC preparation:

COMPARATIVE ANALYSIS OF PARLIAMENTARY SYSTEMS: CONSTITUTIONAL VS. ADMINISTRATIVE BODIES, AND THE DICHOTOMY OF LAW AND ORDER AND LAW ENFORCEMENT

Feature/ Criteria	Parliamentary Systems	Constitutional (Elected Bodies)	Administrative Bodies	Law and Order	Law Enforcement
Function	Decision-making body at the national or regional level, which debates and enacts legislation.	Bodies established through the constitution, often elected, to perform certain governance roles.	Typically non-elected bodies, implementing and overseeing government policies and public services.	Refers to the condition of a society in which laws are obeyed, and social and institutional order is maintained.	Bodies and agencies responsible for ensuring that the laws and regulations of a region are followed.
Examples	Lok Sabha and Rajya Sabha in India, House of Commons in the UK.	U.S. Congress, Indian President and Parliament.	Bureaucracy, civil services, public sector units.	Rule of law, social harmony.	Police departments, Central Bureau of Investigation (India), FBI (USA).
Similarities	Both are pillars of democratic governance and are formed for public service.	Both have roles in legislative processes and governance.	Both are part of the executive arm of governance.	Both are concerned with maintaining societal harmony and public safety.	

Feature/ Criteria	Parliamentary Systems	Constitutional (Elected Bodies)	Administrative Bodies	Law and Order	Law Enforcement
Differences	The Parliament is the supreme legislative body, while elected bodies can exist at different tiers of governance (local to national).	Elected bodies derive authority from elections, while administrative bodies are often appointed or employed based on expertise or civil exams.	Law and order is a state or condition, while law enforcement involves active efforts by agencies.		
Togetherness	The parliament is an example of an elected body.	Administrative bodies work under the direction of elected bodies to implement policies and decisions.	Law enforcement agencies work to maintain law and order.		
Influencers	Public opinion, media, lobbying groups, party leadership.	Public opinion, media, party ideologies, lobbying groups.	Policy directions set by elected bodies, public needs, international standards in some cases.	Socio-economic conditions, public sentiment, effectiveness of law enforcement.	Government policies, social issues, technology, international collaboration.

Notes:

1. **Parliamentary Systems** typically refer to the manner in which the legislative and executive branches of government are organized, especially in democracies.

2. **Constitutional (Elected Bodies)** can span from the President, Congress, Parliament to local elected officials like mayors or panchayat leaders.

3. **Administrative Bodies** are typically part of the executive branch, responsible for implementing the decisions made by elected officials.

4. **Law and Order** is more of a concept and condition, whereas **Law Enforcement** is about the actual apparatus and actions taken to maintain that condition.

COMPARATIVE ANALYSIS OF INDIA'S PARLIAMENTARY STRUCTURES: CONSTITUTIONAL BODIES VS. ADMINISTRATIVE ENTITIES, AND THE DYNAMICS OF LAW AND ORDER VS. LAW ENFORCEMENT

Certainly! Let's delve into the specifics of the Indian context to better understand these categories. Here's a table that critically analyses the differences, similarities, togetherness, and influencers for each of these categories in India:

Feature/ Criteria	Parliamentary Systems (India)	Constitutional (Elected Bodies) (India)	Administrative Bodies (India)	Law and Order (India)	Law Enforcement (India)
Function	Primary legislative body, responsible for debating and enacting legislation.	Bodies constituted by the constitution that are elected to serve particular governance roles.	Implement and manage government policies, services, and public administration.	Refers to the societal state where laws are adhered to, ensuring stability and peace.	Bodies and organizations mandated to ensure that laws and regulations are upheld.
Examples	Lok Sabha and Rajya Sabha.	President of India, State Legislative Assemblies, Panchayats, Municipalities.	IAS, IPS, IFS officers, central and state government departments.	Maintenance of peace during elections, public gatherings.	Police departments, Central Bureau of Investigation, CRPF.
Similarities	Both are key components of governance and democratic processes in India.	Both execute and manage the policies and decisions of elected officials.	Both aim at preserving societal harmony and public welfare.		

Feature/ Criteria	Parliamentary Systems (India)	Constitutional (Elected Bodies) (India)	Administrative Bodies (India)	Law and Order (India)	Law Enforcement (India)
Differences	Lok Sabha members are directly elected, while Rajya Sabha members are elected by elected members of State Assemblies.	Elected bodies derive power from the people, while administrative bodies are usually selected based on expertise or exams like the UPSC.	Law and order is a broader concept related to societal stability, while law enforcement is about the agencies and actions taken to ensure that stability.		
Togetherness	The Parliament is an epitome of an elected body at the national level.	Administrative bodies work as per the guidance of elected bodies to ensure policy implementation.	Law enforcement agencies function to ensure and enhance law and order.		
Influencers	Public sentiment, media, party leadership, lobbying groups.	Voter base, party ideologies, media, lobbying groups.	Directives set by elected officials, public needs, global standards in some areas.	Economic factors, public sentiment, effectiveness of law enforcement agencies.	Government policies, societal concerns, technology, public sentiment, judiciary decisions.

Notes:

1. **Parliamentary Systems in India**: Comprise both the Houses of the Parliament - Lok Sabha (House of the People) and Rajya Sabha (Council of States). They play a pivotal role in the legislative processes.

2. **Constitutional (Elected Bodies) in India**: Span from the President to local elected bodies like Panchayats. These bodies derive their authority from the Constitution of India and the electoral mandate.

3. **Administrative Bodies in India**: Consist of the bureaucracy and other allied services which play a vital role in the day-to-day administration and policy implementation.

4. **Law and Order in India**: It's a state subject, meaning that each state has its own apparatus and policies, albeit within the broader framework of the Indian Constitution.

5. **Law Enforcement in India**: While police are primarily a state subject, there are central law enforcement agencies, like the CBI or the CRPF, that operate under the jurisdiction of the central government.

A CRITICAL EVALUATION: DISTINGUISHING AND BRIDGING INDIA'S PARLIAMENTARY SYSTEMS, CONSTITUTIONAL VS. ADMINISTRATIVE BODIES, AND THE NUANCES OF LAW AND ORDER VS. LAW ENFORCEMENT

Absolutely, let's delve into a critical evaluation of these systems, specifically in the Indian context:

1. Parliamentary Systems:

Nature: Legislative, decision-making body. **Features:** Comprises two houses in India – Lok Sabha (House of the People) and Rajya Sabha (Council of States).

- **Differences:** Lok Sabha members are directly elected, whereas Rajya Sabha members are elected by elected members of State Assemblies.

- **Influencers:** Party politics, lobbyists, public sentiment, international events, media.

2. Constitutional (Elected Bodies):

Nature: Elected, representational entities instituted by the Constitution. **Features:** Include the President of India, State Legislative Assemblies, Panchayats, and Municipalities.

- **Differences:** Vary in powers, jurisdiction, and election processes. For example, the President is elected by an electoral college, while members of State Assemblies are directly elected by citizens.

- **Influencers:** Local issues, political parties, public sentiment, media coverage.

3. Administrative Bodies:

Nature: Executive entities that implement policies and provide services. **Features:** Comprise the bureaucracy (like IAS, IPS, IFS officers) and other government departments.

- **Differences:** While both are part of the executive branch, elected bodies create/direct policy, and administrative bodies implement and manage it.

- **Influencers:** Policy guidelines, directives from elected bodies, public feedback, international standards/agreements.

4. Law and Order:

Nature: The societal state in which laws are followed and stability is ensured. **Features:** Pertains to the conditions ensuring peace, security, and stability in society.

- **Differences:** Law and order is a broader societal condition, while law enforcement is an active process to ensure this state.

- **Influencers:** Societal norms, economic conditions, political stability, public trust in institutions.

5. Law Enforcement:

Nature: Agencies and actions taken to uphold laws. **Features:** Includes police departments, Central Bureau of Investigation (CBI), CRPF, and other security agencies.

- **Differences:** Their jurisdiction, powers, and areas of expertise vary.

- **Influencers:** Legal framework, government policies, public sentiment, judiciary, media.

Evaluation:

- **Interrelation:** Elected bodies pass laws and policies, administrative bodies execute them, and law enforcement ensures compliance. All these function within the framework of law and order.

- **Dependence:** Law enforcement agencies need legal backing (from parliamentary systems) to operate. Simultaneously, elected and administrative bodies rely on law enforcement to ensure that their directives are followed.

- **Potential Conflicts:** Elected bodies might pass populist policies to gain public favor, sometimes sacrificing long-term benefits. Administrative bodies might face bureaucratic red-tapism, potentially slowing down policy implementation. Law enforcement, while aiming for strict adherence to rules, might sometimes be viewed as oppressive, especially if they're misused by powerful entities.

♦ **Checks & Balances:** In a well-functioning democracy like India, these systems keep each other in check. The judiciary plays a vital role in ensuring that no single entity oversteps its bounds.

To understand them critically:

1. **Parliamentary systems** provide the foundation for democratic governance but can sometimes be bogged down by partisan politics.

2. **Elected bodies** provide representation but might often engage in populism.

3. **Administrative bodies** offer stability but can be slow and mired in red tape.

4. **Law and order** is a barometer for societal health but can be fragile.

5. **Law enforcement** ensures compliance but can become over-authoritarian if not checked.

The interplay between these categories is the cornerstone of governance in India. Proper functioning hinges on the delicate balance of power, responsibility, and accountability between them.

SYNCHRONIZED GOVERNANCE: HOW UPSC, STATE BODIES, AND RECRUITING AGENCIES ENSURE COHESIVE AND SECURE POWER TRANSITIONS ACROSS INDIA'S ADMINISTRATIVE LEVELS

The Union Public Service Commission (UPSC) and its state-level counterparts are critical in maintaining administrative continuity, ensuring harmonious power transfer, and preserving the meritocratic structure of India's bureaucracy. Their role in recruitment ensures that public administration remains largely immune to the transient nature of political power and its associated changes.

Let's delve into how these recruitment bodies play a role in creating harmony and ensuring safe power transfer across various administrative levels:

1. **Local, Panchayat, and Mandal Level:**

    ◆ **Recruitment:** State Public Service Commissions (PSCs) or Subordinate Selection Boards often oversee recruitment for positions at these levels.

    ◆ **Harmony through Professionalism:** By recruiting competent and impartial individuals, the administrative machinery at these grassroots levels functions effectively. Such professionalism ensures that local governance remains stable despite potential political changes or local disputes.

    ◆ **Neutral Administration:** The bureaucracy at these levels acts as a neutral entity, focusing on policy implementation rather than political affiliation.

2. **Divisional and District Level:**

    ◆ **Recruitment:** Many officers, especially in the administrative and police services at these levels, are recruited through state PSCs or the UPSC.

- **Continuity:** District Collectors/Magistrates, Superintendents of Police, and other pivotal roles often serve as binding forces during power transitions, ensuring that administrative functions continue smoothly.

- **Conflict Resolution:** These officers play a crucial role in mediating conflicts, ensuring communal harmony, and maintaining peace, especially during elections or political power shifts.

3. State Level:

- **Recruitment:** Senior positions, such as those in the upper echelons of state administration or police, might be filled through promotions, but the initial recruitment often takes place through state PSCs or the UPSC.

- **Stability:** By maintaining a cadre of professionally trained officers, states ensure that the administrative machinery remains functional and non-partisan, irrespective of political changes.

- **Bridging the Gap:** The bureaucracy at the state level plays an essential role in harmonizing state policies with central directives. They act as intermediaries, ensuring that power transitions at the state level do not disrupt this balance.

4. Central Level:

- **Recruitment:** UPSC is the primary body for recruiting officers to central services, such as the Indian Administrative Service (IAS), Indian Police Service (IPS), and Indian Foreign Service (IFS), among others.

- **National Harmony:** Officers, especially from services like the IAS or IPS, are often posted outside their home states. This ensures that they maintain a pan-Indian perspective, promoting national integration and harmony.

- **Safe Power Transfer:** Central-level bureaucrats play a crucial role during national elections and power transitions. They ensure the machinery of governance, from logistics to law and order, functions seamlessly.

Conclusion:

The recruitment process, upheld by UPSC and state PSCs, is rigorous, ensuring that only meritorious candidates enter the administrative services. This meritocracy, combined with tenure security, ensures that officers can execute their duties without undue political pressure. The continuity provided by the bureaucracy is pivotal during political transitions, ensuring that changes in power do not lead to administrative chaos. By acting as neutral agents dedicated to policy implementation, these officers bridge the gap between changing political leaderships and the constant machinery of governance.

EXPLORING THE ROLES IN CSE NOTIFICATIONS: THEIR CONTEMPORARY INFLUENCE AND RELEVANCE IN TODAY'S GOVERNANCE LANDSCAPE

The Civil Services Examination (CSE) conducted by the Union Public Service Commission (UPSC) is one of India's most prestigious exams. It's designed to recruit officers for various services that play crucial roles in the governance and administration of the country. While the specific list of services and posts can vary slightly from one notification to another, the following are generally included:

1. **Indian Administrative Service (IAS):**

   - **Role:** Serve at the helm of public administration at both central and state levels. They handle affairs of government, including framing and implementation of policy in consultation with the concerned minister.

   - **Significance:** The IAS officers play a pivotal role in maintaining administrative continuity in the country. They're central to policy implementation and governance.

2. **Indian Police Service (IPS):**

   - **Role:** They lead and command the Indian police forces, handle law and order, and combat crime.

   - **Significance:** Essential for maintaining law and order in the country, IPS officers often find themselves at the forefront during critical situations, ensuring public safety.

3. **Indian Foreign Service (IFS):**

   - **Role:** Represent India at the international level, manage foreign relations, and serve in international organizations and embassies.

   - **Significance:** They play a central role in diplomacy, international trade negotiations, and maintaining India's foreign relations.

4. **Indian Revenue Service (IRS - Income Tax & Customs):**

   ♦ **Role:** Manage and administer direct and indirect taxations, respectively.

   ♦ **Significance:** Central to revenue collection, which is crucial for the nation's financial health.

5. **Indian Audit and Accounts Service (IAAS):**

   ♦ **Role:** Serve as the guardians of public purse and oversee government spending.

   ♦ **Significance:** They ensure financial accountability and transparency in government operations.

6. **Indian Civil Accounts Service (ICAS):**

   ♦ **Role:** Handle the accounts of the government of India.

   ♦ **Significance:** Play an important role in financial management.

7. **Indian Railway Traffic Service (IRTS):**

   ♦ **Role:** Manage transportation of passengers and freight by railways.

   ♦ **Significance:** Ensure smooth and efficient operation of one of the world's largest rail networks.

8. **Indian Railway Accounts Service (IRAS):**

   ♦ **Role:** Oversee financial matters related to the railways.

   ♦ **Significance:** Play a role in maintaining the financial health of the railways.

... and several other services.

Relevance in Today's Context:

♦ **Significance:** The roles filled by these services are fundamental to the functioning of a vast and diverse country like India. From urban planning, policy implementation, maintaining law and order, to representing India on the global stage, these roles have only grown in significance given the increasing complexities of modern governance.

- **Evolving Challenges:** With new challenges like cybercrime, international trade disputes, environmental concerns, and more, these services continuously evolve, adapt, and upgrade their skill sets.

- **Digital Transformation:** The need for digital governance, e-services, and technology-driven solutions means that officers are also navigating new tools and platforms, underlining their continued relevance.

The Civil Services Examination (CSE) conducted by the Union Public Service Commission (UPSC) recruits for a wide range of Central services. The following is an exhaustive list of services that aspirants can be allotted to based on their rank and preference:

1. **Indian Administrative Service (IAS)**

2. **Indian Foreign Service (IFS)**

3. **Indian Police Service (IPS)**

4. **Indian Revenue Service (IRS) - Income Tax**

5. **Indian Revenue Service (IRS) - Customs and Central Excise**

6. **Indian Audit and Accounts Service (IAAS)**

7. **Indian Defence Accounts Service (IDAS)**

8. **Indian Civil Accounts Service (ICAS)**

9. **Indian Corporate Law Service (ICLS)**

10. **Indian Railway Traffic Service (IRTS)**

11. **Indian Railway Accounts Service (IRAS)**

12. **Indian Railway Personnel Service (IRPS)**

13. **Indian Defence Estates Service (IDES)**

14. **Indian Information Service (IIS)**

15. **Indian Trade Service (ITS)**

16. **Indian P&T Accounts and Finance Service**

17. **Indian Postal Service**

18. **Indian Ordnance Factories Service (IOFS)**

19. **Indian Telecommunication Service**

20. **Armed Forces Headquarters Civil Services**

21. **Delhi, Andaman and Nicobar Islands Civil Service (DANICS)**

22. **Delhi, Andaman and Nicobar Islands Police Service (DANIPS)**

23. **Central Secretariat Service (CSS)**

24. **Central Secretariat Stenographers' Service**

25. **Customs Preliminary Service (renamed as Assistant in Customs) - now a feeder service**

The significance and roles of each service vary, but they are all critical to the functioning of the government and administration at various levels.

In conclusion, while the context, tools, and challenges faced by the civil services might evolve, their inherent significance in the structure of Indian governance remains as vital today as it ever was.

Note: The above list is exhaustive as of my last training data up until September 2021. There may have been minor changes or additions to the list of services recruited through the CSE since then. Always refer to the official UPSC notification for the most accurate and up-to-date list.

THE ENDURING IMPACT: UNPACKING THE SIGNIFICANCE OF EACH ROLE IN CSE NOTIFICATIONS IN TODAY'S CONTEXT

Absolutely, each service and post recruited through the Civil Services Examination (CSE) has its distinct significance in the context of governance and administration. Here's a breakdown of the significance of each:

1. **Indian Administrative Service (IAS):**
   - **Role:** At the forefront of public administration at both central and state levels.
   - **Current Significance:** Provides administrative continuity, plays a central role in policy framing, implementation, and disaster management. They have been critical in managing health crises, natural disasters, and digital governance initiatives.

2. **Indian Foreign Service (IFS):**
   - **Role:** Represents India internationally.
   - **Current Significance:** In the context of a globalized world, diplomacy, international trade negotiations, and representation in global organizations are key. The IFS ensures India's stance is effectively communicated and negotiated at international forums.

3. **Indian Police Service (IPS):**
   - **Role:** Law and order maintenance.
   - **Current Significance:** Critical for internal security, counter-terrorism, cybercrime prevention, and public safety. With evolving threats, the role of the IPS is more vital than ever.

4. Indian Revenue Services (IRS - Income Tax & Customs):

♦ **Role:** Taxation and revenue collection.

♦ **Current Significance:** Ensures financial health of the nation by curbing tax evasion, combating financial fraud, and implementing economic reforms.

5. Indian Audit and Accounts Service (IAAS):

♦ **Role:** Audits government spending.

♦ **Current Significance:** Financial accountability and ensuring transparency in governmental financial operations.

6. Indian Defence Accounts Service (IDAS):

♦ **Role:** Manages defense accounts.

♦ **Current Significance:** Ensures transparent and efficient utilization of the defense budget, which is vital for national security.

7. Indian Civil Accounts Service (ICAS):

♦ **Role:** Manages public accounts.

♦ **Current Significance:** Handles the financial administration, ensuring the government's resources are used effectively.

8. Indian Corporate Law Service (ICLS):

♦ **Role:** Regulates corporate sector according to law.

♦ **Current Significance:** Ensures corporate accountability, especially vital with increasing corporate frauds and the need for business regulation.

9. Indian Railway Services (IRTS, IRAS, IRPS):

♦ **Role:** Oversee India's railway operations, finances, and personnel.

♦ **Current Significance:** Railways are crucial for transportation and commerce. Their efficient management, especially in initiatives like the bullet train or metro projects, is essential.

10. Indian Defence Estates Service (IDES):

- **Role:** Civilian officers under the Ministry of Defence managing the Cantonments and Defence Estates.

- **Current Significance:** Ensures land resources for defense purposes are managed and maintained effectively.

11. Indian Information Service (IIS):

- **Role:** Media and public communication for the government.

- **Current Significance:** In an age of information, they manage government communications, ensuring transparency and clear communication of government initiatives.

12. Indian Trade Service (ITS):

- **Role:** Deals with foreign trade.

- **Current Significance:** In a globalized economy, managing trade agreements, trade disputes, and export-import policies are of paramount importance.

13. Indian P&T Accounts and Finance Service:

- **Role:** Financial management in telecom and postal sectors.

- **Current Significance:** With the growth in telecommunications and digital infrastructure, their role in financial oversight is crucial.

14. Indian Postal Service:

- **Role:** Administer postal services.

- **Current Significance:** Beyond traditional mail, the service now plays a role in financial inclusion through postal banking and other services.

15. Indian Ordnance Factories Service (IOFS):

- **Role:** Manages Indian Ordnance Factories.

- **Current Significance:** Ensures the Indian military has the equipment and ordnance it needs.

16. Indian Telecommunication Service:

- **Role:** Administrative service related to telecommunications.

- **Current Significance:** In the digital age, managing and expanding India's telecommunication infrastructure is crucial.

17. Armed Forces Headquarters Civil Services:

- **Role:** Civilian officers who assist in administration at the Armed Forces Headquarters.

- **Current Significance:** Provides administrative support ensuring smooth operations.

18. Delhi, Andaman and Nicobar Islands Civil Service (DANICS) & Police Service (DANIPS):

- **Role:** Administrative and police service for the Union Territories.

- **Current Significance:** Manage affairs in UTs ensuring governance in these strategic and culturally unique regions.

19. Central Secretariat Services:

- **Role:** Provides administrative support to the Central government.

- **Current Significance:** Ensures effective functioning of various departments in the central government.

20. Customs Preliminary Service (now a feeder service):

- **Role:** Junior-level officers in customs.

- **Current Significance:** They play a role in import/export regulation, crucial for India's international trade.

The evolving challenges of modern governance, from cyber threats and international diplomacy to economic reforms and digital transformation, mean that each of these services remains highly relevant. The officers of these services adapt to changing circumstances, ensuring the effective administration and governance of the nation.

COLONIAL LEGACIES IN POST-INDEPENDENCE INDIA: A CRITICAL EXAMINATION OF PERSISTING INFLUENCES AND THEIR IMPLICATIONS

The criticism that post-independence India continues to be influenced by colonial-era policies is a prominent discourse in academic and political circles. It raises valid concerns about the degree to which colonial-era frameworks, institutions, and practices still play a role in modern-day India. Let's critically evaluate this assertion:

Colonial Influences in Post-Independence India:

1. **Bureaucratic Structure**: The Indian Administrative Service (IAS), Indian Police Service (IPS), and other services were derived from colonial administrative services like the Indian Civil Service (ICS) and the Indian Police. While they were renamed and reformed post-independence, the foundational structures and certain practices have their origins in the British era.

2. **Legal Framework**: The Indian Penal Code (IPC) of 1860, the Criminal Procedure Code (CrPC), and several other laws that are still in effect today were created during the British era. While many of them have been amended, their foundational principles remain.

3. **Railways and Infrastructure**: Much of India's railway system, roadways, and other key infrastructures were initiated during the British rule. While they have been expanded and modernized since independence, the base was colonial.

4. **Education System**: The structure of India's education system, especially higher education, finds its roots in colonial policies. The emphasis on English as a medium of instruction in many institutions is a legacy of the British era.

5. **Land Revenue Systems**: Land revenue systems, like the Zamindari, Ryotwari, and Mahalwari, were implemented by the British. Post-

independence, while there were efforts to abolish the Zamindari system, some remnants of these land revenue systems persist in parts of India.

Reasons for Continuation:

1. **Continuity and Stability**: Abrupt changes in administrative or legal systems could have led to chaos in the immediate aftermath of independence. The decision to continue with certain colonial-era frameworks was often a practical one.

2. **Legitimacy**: Some structures, like the judicial system or the railways, were seen as efficient and legitimate, making it logical to continue with them with necessary reforms.

3. **Resource Constraints**: Building entirely new structures or systems requires resources – both human and financial. Post-independence India had other pressing priorities like resettling refugees, integrating princely states, and setting up a democratic framework.

Counterpoints:

1. **Democratic Deepening**: While India retained certain colonial structures, it also undertook profound democratic reforms. The establishment of universal adult suffrage, reservation policies, and decentralization of power through Panchayati Raj institutions are examples.

2. **Socio-Economic Reforms**: The post-independence era saw significant land reforms, the nationalization of key industries, and the adoption of a socialist approach, which were departures from colonial policies.

3. **Cultural Revival and Autonomy**: Efforts to promote regional languages, the reorganization of states on linguistic lines, and promotion of indigenous art and culture were a shift away from colonial legacies.

4. **Legal Reforms**: Over the decades, many archaic British-era laws have been repealed or significantly amended to suit the needs of independent India.

Conclusion:

While it's undeniable that certain colonial legacies persist in post-independence India, it's essential to recognize the nuanced ways in which India has transformed these structures, retained some for practical purposes, and discarded or reformed others. The journey of independent India is one of navigating this complex legacy, balancing the need for continuity with the demands of a sovereign, democratic, and diverse nation.

THE DYNAMICS OF POLITICAL INFLUENCE ON CIVIL SERVANTS IN INDIA: A COMPREHENSIVE ANALYSIS AND PERSPECTIVE VALIDATION

The criticism of political influence on civil servants in India is a topic that has garnered significant attention over the years. The crux of the criticism lies in the perceived erosion of the neutrality of the civil services due to political interference. Let's delve deeper into this criticism, understand its context, and evaluate its validity:

Criticism:

1. **Transfers and Postings**: Frequent transfers of civil servants, especially those who take actions against vested political interests, are often cited as evidence of political interference. A premature transfer can disrupt continuity in administration and demotivate upright officers.

2. **Political Patronage**: Some argue that certain civil servants who align with the political views of the ruling party receive preferential treatment, key postings, or post-retirement appointments.

3. **Policy Implementation**: There's a perception that policies or schemes are sometimes implemented with an eye on electoral gains rather than genuine public welfare. Civil servants may be pressured to focus on these schemes, sometimes at the cost of other vital projects.

4. **Erosion of Autonomy**: Instances where advice from the civil services is overridden or ignored by political executives raise concerns about the diminishing autonomy and influence of expert civil servants in policymaking.

Counterarguments:

1. **Democratic Control**: In a democracy, elected representatives are accountable to the public. Civil servants, being non-elected, are required to

operate under the direction of these elected representatives. This hierarchy ensures the primacy of democratic accountability.

2. **Checks and Balances**: There are institutional checks and balances in place. Bodies like the Central Administrative Tribunal (CAT), courts, and mechanisms like the Right to Information Act provide avenues for civil servants to address grievances and ensure transparency.

3. **Civil Service Integrity**: While instances of political interference do exist, the vast majority of the civil service continues to function with integrity and commitment. Many officers uphold the rule of law and the principles of the Constitution, even in the face of challenges.

4. **Adaptive Measures**: Over the years, several states have introduced measures like minimum fixed tenures for postings to reduce arbitrary transfers. The Central government too has periodically emphasized the need for stability in tenures.

Differentiating Factor:

The Indian civil services, rooted in the colonial era, were envisioned as an impartial body, insulated from political pressures. This vision, although tested, still differentiates India from many countries where partisan civil services change with every new regime. The meritocratic entry and the career progression based on seniority (with limited performance-based assessment) ensure a degree of neutrality.

Conclusion:

While the criticism of political influence on civil servants in India holds some merit, it's essential to view it in the broader context of a democratic framework where elected representatives have a mandate to govern. It's also crucial to recognize the resilience of the civil services and their continuing role in upholding constitutional values. The challenge lies in ensuring that the delicate balance between democratic control and bureaucratic autonomy is maintained for efficient and impartial governance.

FROM BUREAUCRACY TO POLITICS? A REALISTIC EVALUATION OF THE ALLEGED POLITICAL LEANINGS OF CIVIL SERVANTS IN INDIA

Civil servants in India are expected to be neutral and impartial administrators who execute policies and decisions made by the elected representatives. However, there's a criticism that, in some instances, civil servants act more like "political servants" than neutral administrators. Let's critically evaluate this assertion using a realistic approach:

Criticism:

1. **Alignment with Political Interests**: Some civil servants are accused of aligning their administrative decisions with the interests of the ruling political party to curry favor and secure prestigious postings or post-retirement benefits.

2. **Bypassing Established Procedures**: In trying to please political bosses, there have been accusations against some civil servants of bypassing established norms, rules, and procedures.

3. **Partisan Actions**: There are instances where civil servants have been accused of taking sides during politically sensitive events or disputes.

4. **Post-Retirement Benefits**: The lure of post-retirement postings, especially in quasi-judicial bodies, commissions, or tribunals, can be a potential conflict of interest, making some civil servants more amenable to political influence.

Validation and Realistic Assessment:

1. **Nature of Democracy**: In a democracy, it's natural for the bureaucracy to implement the vision and directives of the elected representatives. This might sometimes be perceived as being "political," but it could also be seen as the bureaucracy being responsive to the democratic mandate.

2. **Institutional Mechanisms**: India has strong institutional mechanisms like the Central Vigilance Commission (CVC), Central Administrative Tribunal (CAT), and the courts which can take cognizance of any malpractice. If a civil servant is truly acting as a "political servant," these mechanisms can act as checks.

3. **Public Perception**: In some cases, public perception might not align with the ground reality. An officer acting on genuine administrative grounds might be seen as favoring a political entity due to the inherent controversial nature of certain decisions. Realistically, not every decision that aligns with a political party's interest is taken due to pressure or favoritism.

4. **Training and Orientation**: The Lal Bahadur Shastri National Academy of Administration (LBSNAA) and other training institutions emphasize ethical governance, neutrality, and a commitment to constitutional values. This foundational training equips civil servants to distinguish between political directives and constitutional duties.

5. **Diverse Experiences**: The All India Services and Central Services officers serve across various states and central departments throughout their careers. Exposure to different political landscapes and ideologies acts as a natural deterrent to becoming too aligned with any particular political viewpoint.

6. **Counterexamples**: For every accusation of a civil servant acting politically, there are multiple examples of officers standing their ground, resisting undue political pressures, and upholding the rule of law and principles of justice.

Conclusion:

While the criticism exists and there might be some merit to it in isolated cases, painting the entire civil service with a broad brush isn't realistic. The vast majority of civil servants in India work with dedication, often in challenging conditions, upholding the principles of the Constitution and the rule of law. It's crucial to differentiate between individual aberrations and systemic issues. The framework of checks and balances, coupled with the ethical foundation of the civil services, ensures that the spirit of neutral and efficient administration remains intact in the face of any challenges.

"RED TAPISM" AND NATIONAL PROGRESS: A DETAILED EXAMINATION OF ITS IMPACT ON INDIA'S GROWTH AND DEVELOPMENT

"Red tapism" is a term that signifies excessive bureaucracy, prolonged procedures, and unnecessary rules and regulations that create a hindrance in swift decision-making and effective governance. It's a criticism often levied against the administrative machinery of various countries, including India. Let's critically evaluate the claim that "red tapism" is a significant roadblock for the growth and development of the nation.

Criticism:

1. **Delays in Approvals**: Red tapism can lead to significant delays in acquiring necessary permits, licenses, and approvals for projects. This can deter investors and delay infrastructural and development projects.

2. **Inefficiencies in Governance**: Excessive bureaucracy can slow down the decision-making process, leading to inefficiencies in governance. It can make the administrative machinery less responsive to emerging needs and situations.

3. **Increased Costs**: Delays and uncertainties due to bureaucratic hurdles can increase the cost of projects, making them economically unviable or leading to cost overruns.

4. **Corruption**: Red tapism can sometimes provide fertile ground for corrupt practices. When there are multiple clearances required, it can lead to rent-seeking behavior among officials.

5. **Stifling Innovation**: Entrepreneurs and startups might find it challenging to navigate a complex bureaucratic maze, potentially stifling innovation and business growth.

6. **Impact on Foreign Investment**: Investors often seek predictability and ease of doing business. A reputation for red tapism can deter foreign investments, which are crucial for economic growth.

Validation:

1. **Global Rankings**: India's ranking on the World Bank's Ease of Doing Business index can be an indicator. While India made significant progress in recent years (jumping to the 63rd position in 2020 from 142nd in 2014), there are still areas like enforcing contracts and registering property where the country ranks low, suggesting bureaucratic hurdles.

2. **Testimonies from the Business Community**: Domestic and international businesses have often cited bureaucratic delays as challenges in their operations in India.

3. **Project Delays**: Numerous infrastructural projects in India, from highways to power plants, have faced delays due to a myriad of clearances. These delays translate to increased costs and lost opportunities for economic growth.

4. **Reform Initiatives**: The very fact that successive governments have introduced reforms to cut down red tape indicates its presence and acknowledged impact on growth. Initiatives like the Single Window Clearance system for various projects are a response to the challenges posed by red tapism.

Counterpoints:

1. **Necessary Oversight**: Some procedures and regulations are crucial to ensure that projects meet environmental, social, and safety standards. What might be seen as "red tape" might be necessary oversight in certain contexts.

2. **Improvements Over Time**: With digitalization and e-governance initiatives, many processes that were once time-consuming have become streamlined. Efforts like the Goods and Services Tax (GST) aim to simplify complex tax structures.

3. **Decentralization of Power**: Decentralization, giving more powers to state and local governments, can make processes swifter as local bodies might have a better understanding of regional contexts.

Conclusion:

There's merit to the criticism that red tapism can be a roadblock for growth and development. However, it's also essential to recognize that all bureaucratic procedures aren't unnecessary impediments. Some are vital for ensuring that growth is sustainable, equitable, and doesn't compromise safety or environmental standards. The challenge lies in differentiating necessary oversight from genuine red tape and streamlining processes to make governance more efficient and responsive.

FROM SELECTION TO SERVICE: CHARTING THE PATH OF TRAINING, LEARNING, AND PRACTICAL ACCLIMATIZATION FOR CSE APPOINTEES IN INDIA

After clearing the Civil Services Examination (CSE) conducted by the Union Public Service Commission (UPSC) and being allocated to various services based on rank and preference, successful candidates undergo rigorous training. This training is designed to equip them with the necessary skills, knowledge, and values to discharge their responsibilities effectively.

Here's an elaborate breakdown of the post-selection journey of a civil servant:

1. Foundation Course:

All successful candidates, irrespective of the service they're allocated to, initially undergo a common Foundation Course.

Venue: The primary training institute for this is the **Lal Bahadur Shastri National Academy of Administration (LBSNAA)**, Mussoorie. Some candidates might also be trained at other academies due to the large number of trainees.

Duration: About 15 weeks.

Content: This course covers a wide range of subjects like law, political science, public administration, and management. It also includes modules on soft skills, physical training, extracurricular activities, and treks to build camaraderie among officers of different services.

2. Professional Training:

After the Foundation Course, officers are sent to different training institutes based on the service they've been allocated.

- **Indian Administrative Service (IAS)**: Officers continue their training at **LBSNAA**. This phase includes district training, which gives them a grassroots view of administration.

- **Indian Police Service (IPS)**: The **Sardar Vallabhbhai Patel National Police Academy** in Hyderabad is the venue. Training includes modules on law enforcement, internal security, forensic science, and fieldcraft, among others.

- **Indian Foreign Service (IFS)**: Officers are trained at the **Foreign Service Institute** in New Delhi. They learn about international relations, trade and economics, international law, and also undergo language training.

- **Indian Revenue Service (IRS)**, Customs and Direct Tax: Training happens at the **National Academy of Direct Taxes** in Nagpur for Direct Tax and at **National Academy of Customs, Excise, and Narcotics** in Faridabad for Customs.

- **Other Services**: There are specific academies for other services too, such as the **Indian Railway Management Service**, **Indian Audit and Accounts Service**, etc., where specialized training is imparted.

3. On-the-Job Training:

- **District Training for IAS**: After their professional training at LBSNAA, IAS officers are attached to a district in their cadre state for practical on-the-job training. This is a crucial phase where they learn the practical aspects of administration, working as Sub-Divisional Magistrates.

- **Attachments**: Officers from various services are attached to different departments/agencies (like the Army, BSF, CRPF for IPS officers) for short durations to understand their functions.

4. Mid-Career Training:

To ensure that officers' skills remain updated, there are mid-career training programs. These are organized at different stages of an officer's career, allowing them to learn about the latest developments in administration, technology, and management.

5. Foreign Training:

Officers might also get opportunities to undergo training or attend courses in foreign institutions as part of their service. These stints allow them to understand global best practices and bring those learnings to India.

Conclusion:

Training for civil servants is a continuous and dynamic process. The blend of classroom instruction with practical on-the-job training ensures that they're well-equipped to handle the challenges of their job. The emphasis is not just on professional skills but also on inculcating the right values and ethics essential for public service.

REMUNERATION AND CAREER PROGRESSION OF CIVIL SERVANTS IN INDIA: A DEEP DIVE INTO SALARIES, PROMOTIONAL PATHWAYS, EVALUATION MECHANISMS, AND ADDITIONAL BENEFITS

Civil servants in India have a structured pay scale, promotions pathway, and performance evaluation mechanism. Here's a comprehensive overview of their salaries, promotions, performance evaluations, and additional benefits:

1. Salaries:

The salary of civil servants is determined based on the pay scales and pay bands decided by the government, most recently as per the recommendations of the 7th **Central Pay Commission (CPC).**

- **Basic Structure**: The salary consists of a basic pay, a grade pay, and other allowances such as Dearness Allowance (DA), House Rent Allowance (HRA), and Travel Allowance (TA).

- **Starting Salary**: For a new entrant, the salary typically starts at the level of Under Secretary or Assistant Secretary for services like the IAS, IPS, or IFS.

2. Salary Hikes:

- **Annual Increments**: Civil servants receive annual increments based on their performance and the pay matrix's stipulated percentage.

- **Dearness Allowance (DA)**: Adjusted twice a year, the DA compensates for inflation. It's a percentage of the basic pay and can change based on the consumer price index.

3. Promotions:

Promotions for civil servants are structured and occur at regular intervals, subject to satisfactory performance.

- **Time-Based**: After certain years of service, officers are eligible for promotions. For example, an IAS officer starts as a Sub-Divisional Magistrate and can move up to District Collector and further to various Secretarial roles at the state and central levels.

- **Performance-Based**: The performance of officers is periodically evaluated, and this plays a role in their promotions, especially for senior roles.

4. Performance Evaluation:

- **Annual Performance Appraisal Report (APAR)**: It's the primary tool to evaluate an officer's work over the year. The report is written by the immediate superior and reviewed by higher authorities.

- **360-Degree Feedback**: For certain senior-level posts, feedback from subordinates, peers, and superiors might be considered, offering a comprehensive view of an officer's capabilities.

5. Promotional and Engagement Agencies:

- **Departmental Promotion Committees (DPC)**: These committees are set up to evaluate officers for promotions. They consider the APARs and other records to make their decisions.

6. Additional Benefits:

- **Accommodation**: Most officers are provided with government housing based on their rank and location of posting.

- **Official Vehicles**: Depending on the service and rank, officers are entitled to official vehicles.

- **Leave Travel Concession (LTC)**: Officers and their families are eligible for LTC to travel to different parts of the country.

- **Medical Benefits**: Officers have access to medical facilities and benefits.

- **Post-Retirement**: Pension benefits are available post-retirement, and there are provisions for gratuity and other retirement benefits.

- **Study Leave**: Officers can apply for study leave to pursue higher education, often with full pay and allowances.

Additional Benefits:

1. **Accommodation**: Government-provided housing or a housing allowance, often in prime areas of the city or district they're posted in.

2. **Official Vehicles**: Depending on rank and service, officers may be provided with official vehicles, sometimes with chauffeur services.

3. **Leave Travel Concession (LTC)**: Officers and their families are entitled to LTC for travel within India and, in some cases, even abroad.

4. **Medical Benefits**: Comprehensive medical facilities for officers and their immediate families. This includes access to premium government hospitals and reimbursement of medical expenses.

5. **Post-Retirement Benefits**:

    ◆ **Pension**: Lifelong pension, which can also be transferred to the spouse in the event of the officer's demise.

    ◆ **Gratuity**: A lump sum payment upon retirement.

    ◆ **Provident Fund**: Contribution-based savings which are handed over upon retirement.

6. **Study Leave**: Officers can avail study leave to pursue higher education, generally with full pay and allowances. This is especially beneficial for those looking to specialize in certain areas.

7. **Paid Holidays**: Apart from the standard government holidays, officers also have a fixed number of casual and earned leaves.

8. **Security**: Depending on the posting and perceived threat, officers (especially in services like the IAS or IPS) may be provided with personal security.

9. **Club Memberships**: Some officers are granted memberships to prestigious government clubs or institutes, which provide recreational and networking opportunities.

10. **Training Opportunities**: Periodic in-service training, both domestically and internationally, keeping officers updated with the latest in administration, governance, and policy-making.

11. **Telecommunication Allowance**: For certain posts, the government provides an allowance to cover telecommunication expenses.

12. **Children's Education Allowance**: A certain amount is reimbursed for expenses incurred on the education of children.

13. **Hardship Allowance**: Officers posted in challenging terrains or conflict areas might receive additional allowances.

14. **Utility Allowance**: Some officers might receive an allowance to cover utility bills.

Conclusion:

The pay and benefits for civil servants in India are structured to provide stability, growth, and reward performance. Over the years, pay commissions have periodically revised salaries to ensure they're competitive and in line with economic realities. The structured promotion and performance evaluation processes ensure that there's a clear pathway for career growth, rewarding competence and dedication.

The extensive benefits package for civil servants is designed not only as a mark of recognition for their service but also to ensure that they can perform their duties without undue personal or financial stress. These benefits, along with the prestige associated with civil services, make it one of the most sought-after professions in India.

TRAINING ENDEAVORS FOR INDIA'S CIVIL SERVICE POSTS: A COMPREHENSIVE OVERVIEW OF OPPORTUNITIES AND INSTITUTIONS

The training opportunities for various posts and positions in the Indian Civil Services are comprehensive and tailored to each service's unique needs. Here's a breakdown:

1. **Indian Administrative Service (IAS):**

   - **Foundation Course** at the Lal Bahadur Shastri National Academy of Administration (LBSNAA), Mussoorie.

   - **Professional Course Phase I** at LBSNAA.

   - **District Training**: On-the-ground training where officers learn the practical aspects of governance, revenue administration, and development programs.

   - **Professional Course Phase II** at LBSNAA, marking the end of training with a module designed to integrate learnings.

2. **Indian Police Service (IPS):**

   - Training at the **Sardar Vallabhbhai Patel National Police Academy**, Hyderabad.

   - Modules cover law, policing techniques, forensics, cybersecurity, field training, weapons training, and police administration.

   - **Practical Training**: Attachments with various central and state police and paramilitary organizations for hands-on experience.

3. **Indian Foreign Service (IFS):**

   - Training begins at LBSNAA, followed by specialized training at the **Foreign Service Institute (FSI)**, New Delhi.

- Modules cover international relations, trade, India's foreign policy, diplomatic etiquettes, and language training.

- **On-the-Job Training**: Attachments with various ministries, and postings at Indian missions abroad.

4. **Indian Revenue Service (IRS) - Income Tax/CCE:**

    - **National Academy of Direct Taxes (NADT)**, Nagpur for IRS (Income Tax).

    - **National Academy of Customs, Excise, and Narcotics (NACEN)**, Faridabad for IRS (Customs and Central Excise).

    - Modules cover tax laws, fiscal policies, auditing, financial management, and administrative procedures.

5. **Indian Audit and Accounts Service (IA&AS):**

    - Training at the **National Academy of Audit and Accounts**, Shimla.

    - Focuses on public finance, auditing, accountancy, and financial management.

6. **Indian Railway Services (IRTS, IRAS, IRPS, etc.):**

    - Training institutes include **National Academy of Indian Railways**, Vadodara; **Indian Railways Institute of Civil Engineering**, Pune; and others.

    - Training covers rail transport and management, rail infrastructure, and operations.

7. **Indian Forest Service (IFoS):**

    - **Indira Gandhi National Forest Academy (IGNFA)**, Dehradun.

    - Comprehensive training on forestry, wildlife management, environmental laws, and related subjects.

8. **Other Central Services (like IA&AS, IDAS, ITS, etc.):**

    - Each service has its own dedicated training institution focusing on the specific nuances and needs of that service.

9. **Mid-Career Training:**

    - For all services, there are **mid-career training programs** that officers can attend. These are organized at different intervals in an officer's career to update their skills and knowledge.

◆ Some officers may also get opportunities for foreign training, executive courses in global universities, and participation in international conferences.

Conclusion:

Training opportunities in the Indian Civil Services are designed to equip officers with the necessary skills, attitudes, and knowledge to handle their roles effectively. Given the vast scope and responsibility of these services, the training is rigorous, comprehensive, and continuously evolving to address the dynamic nature of administration and governance.

CHARTING THE IDEAL TIMELINE: WHEN TO BEGIN PREPARATION FOR THE CSE?

The right time to start preparing for the Civil Services Examination (CSE) varies from person to person based on their individual strengths, background knowledge, and preparation strategy. However, there are some general considerations:

1. **Undergraduate Years**: Some aspirants begin their preparation during their undergraduate years, especially if they are pursuing courses in arts, humanities, or social sciences which might have some overlap with the UPSC syllabus. Starting early provides an advantage of time, allowing aspirants to understand the vast syllabus and decide their optional subject wisely.

2. **Immediately After Graduation**: A significant number of aspirants choose to start their preparation right after completing their graduation. This is a time when they can devote undivided attention to CSE preparation.

3. **Work and Prepare**: Some individuals begin their preparation while working. They usually allocate a few hours daily for UPSC preparation and may eventually take a break closer to the examination date for intensive study.

4. **Age and Number of Attempts**: The UPSC has age and attempt limits. General category candidates, for instance, have 6 attempts till the age of 32 (with certain exceptions). Other categories have relaxed criteria. Aspirants should keep these limits in mind and plan accordingly.

Factors to Consider:

1. **Individual Strengths**: Some people are quick learners, while others may require more time to grasp topics. Recognizing one's strengths and weaknesses early can help in deciding when to start.

2. **Background Knowledge**: Aspirants with a background in subjects that are part of the UPSC syllabus might find it easier to start. For example, a graduate in political science might be more comfortable with the polity segment of the syllabus.

3. **Coaching or Self-Study**: Those opting for coaching might require a dedicated preparation period after graduation, while those going for self-study might have flexibility in terms of when they start.

4. **Comprehensive Nature of Exam**: Given the vastness of the syllabus and the unpredictable nature of UPSC questions, a longer preparation time might be beneficial.

5. **Multiple Revisions**: The key to success in UPSC is not just understanding but retaining and reproducing vast amounts of information. Starting early allows for multiple revisions, which is crucial for retention.

Conclusion:

While the above points provide a general guideline, it's essential to understand that every aspirant's journey is unique. The "right time" is truly when an individual feels ready and committed to the rigorous preparation process. The most crucial factor is consistency. Whether an aspirant starts early or later, maintaining regularity in preparation and having a strategic approach can make the difference.

Leveraging Individual Strengths: The Key to Unlocking Success in the CSE:

Individual strengths play a significant role in the preparation and success of aspirants in the Civil Services Examination (CSE). Different strengths can be leveraged to enhance the efficiency of preparation, handle the demands of the exam, and maximize performance. Let's discuss how various individual strengths can be beneficial:

1. Analytical Skills:

- Helps in understanding complex issues and topics in the syllabus.
- Useful for answering application-based questions and making logical connections.

2. Memory and Retention:

- With the vast syllabus, the ability to remember and recall facts, dates, and concepts becomes crucial.

- Helps in the Prelims stage, which is largely fact-oriented.

3. Time Management:

- Assists in efficiently covering the extensive syllabus.

- Crucial during the examination to attempt all questions within the stipulated time.

4. Writing Skills:

- Vital for the Mains examination, where presentation, clarity, and coherence in answers can fetch more marks.

- Helps in essay writing and structuring answers effectively.

5. Reading and Comprehension:

- Facilitates understanding of diverse topics from various sources.

- Aids in solving comprehension-based questions in the Prelims and certain papers in Mains.

6. Stress Management and Emotional Resilience:

- Preparing for CSE can be mentally exhausting. The ability to handle stress ensures consistency in preparation.

- Helps maintain composure during the examination and tackle unexpected questions.

7. Self-discipline and Motivation:

- Ensures regularity in studies, minimizing distractions.

- Keeps the aspirant focused during the long preparation phase.

8. Flexibility and Adaptability:

- Helps in switching strategies if something isn't working.

- Allows adapting to the evolving nature of UPSC questions and unpredictability.

9. Interpersonal Skills:

- Useful for group studies and discussions, which can be a great way to gain multiple perspectives on a topic.

- Assists in the Personality Test (Interview) phase, where communication skills, empathy, and sociability are evaluated.

10. Critical Thinking:

- Helps in the analysis of editorials, government policies, and global events.

- Vital for answer writing in the Mains, where critical evaluation of topics is often required.

11. Organizational Skills:

- Aids in organizing notes, resources, and timetables.

- Helps streamline the preparation process.

12. Endurance and Perseverance:

- Ensures aspirants remain committed despite setbacks or failures.

- The CSE journey can be long, and these qualities help maintain the momentum.

Leveraging Individual Strengths:

It's essential for aspirants to recognize their unique strengths early on and develop a preparation strategy that capitalizes on them. At the same time, it's beneficial to work on areas of weakness. For instance, if someone is not naturally inclined towards essay writing, practicing regularly can help improve this skill. Recognizing strengths and using them to one's advantage can make the preparation process more tailored, efficient, and effective.

BUILDING A SOLID FOUNDATION: ESSENTIAL BACKGROUND KNOWLEDGE FOR CSE SUCCESS

The Civil Services Examination (CSE) by UPSC is one of the most diverse exams in terms of the syllabus. Aspirants from varied academic backgrounds, be it arts, science, commerce, engineering, or medicine, compete in this exam. While every academic background has its advantages, some "background knowledge" areas can be particularly helpful. Let's explore:

1. **Indian Polity and Governance:**

    ◆   Understanding the Constitution, political system, Panchayati Raj, public policy, and rights issues.

    ◆   Knowledge of basic political concepts, the structure and functioning of the Indian government at various levels.

2. **History:**

    ◆   Knowledge of ancient, medieval, and modern Indian history, including the national freedom movement.

    ◆   World history, especially events from the 18th century onwards.

3. **Geography:**

    ◆   Basic geographical concepts and terminologies.

    ◆   Physical, economic, and human geography of India and the world.

4. **Economics:**

    ◆   Fundamental economic concepts, including microeconomics and macroeconomics.

    ◆   Indian economy, its structure, and issues related to it.

5. **Environment and Ecology:**

- Environmental concepts, biodiversity, conservation, climate change, and sustainable development.
- Understanding of global environmental issues and treaties.

6. Science and Technology:

- Basic understanding of physics, chemistry, biology, and recent technological advancements.
- Contemporary issues and developments in biotechnology, IT, space, nuclear, and health sectors.

7. Current Affairs:

- Awareness of national and international events.
- Reading newspapers and magazines regularly and comprehensively.

8. Social Issues:

- Knowledge about the social structure, demographics, and pressing issues in Indian society.
- Themes like poverty, unemployment, social sector initiatives, etc.

9. Ethics and Integrity:

- Basic understanding of ethics, values, and public administration.
- Knowledge of thinkers, philosophers, and administrators to answer case-based questions.

10. Statistics and Data Interpretation:

- Basic mathematical ability and data interpretation are essential for certain Preliminary examination questions.

11. International Relations:

- India's foreign policy, international events, and India's relations with different countries and organizations.

How Different Academic Backgrounds Can Help:

- **Arts/Humanities Graduates**: Have a foundational knowledge in subjects like history, political science, and sociology. This aids in the preparation for general studies papers.

- **Science/Engineering Graduates**: Have an analytical approach, which can be advantageous in subjects like geography, environment, and science & technology. Their quantitative aptitude can be useful for certain Prelims questions.

- **Commerce/Economics Graduates**: Have a grounding in economic principles, financial institutions, and Indian economy-related topics.

- **Medical Graduates**: Can leverage their background in topics related to health, biotechnology, and certain aspects of environment and ecology.

Conclusion:

While background knowledge in the areas mentioned above can be advantageous, it's important to note that UPSC is designed to level the playing field for aspirants from all academic backgrounds. Many candidates without any prior knowledge in these areas have successfully cleared the CSE with dedicated preparation and the right strategy.

PATHWAYS TO CSE MASTERY: THE ROLE OF COACHING VS. THE POWER OF SELF-STUDY

The debate between coaching and self-study for the Civil Services Examination (CSE) has been ongoing for years. Both approaches have their advantages and drawbacks. Let's critically examine both to provide clarity:

Coaching:

Advantages:

1. **Structured Learning**: Coaching institutes provide a structured syllabus and study plan, which can help in covering the vast CSE syllabus systematically.

2. **Expert Guidance**: Experienced faculty can explain complex topics in a simplified manner and provide insights that might be hard to glean from textbooks alone.

3. **Regular Assessment**: Regular mock tests and answer writing sessions help in gauging preparation levels and improving exam strategy.

4. **Study Materials**: Institutes often provide condensed notes, which can be beneficial for revision.

5. **Peer Interaction**: Being around other aspirants can be motivating. Group discussions can provide diverse viewpoints on various topics.

6. **Doubt Clearing**: Immediate doubt resolution can speed up the learning process.

Drawbacks:

1. **Expensive**: Coaching can be costly, and not everyone can afford it.

2. **Standardized Approach**: The "one-size-fits-all" approach may not cater to individual needs and learning paces.

3. **Over-reliance**: Some aspirants might become overly dependent on coaching, undermining their self-study efforts.

Self-Study:

Advantages:

1. **Flexibility**: Aspirants can plan their study schedule based on their strengths and weaknesses, and they are not bound by a fixed class timetable.

2. **Personalized Approach**: Aspirants can delve deeper into areas of interest or spend more time on weaker sections.

3. **Cost-effective**: Self-study eliminates coaching fees. The main expenses are books and other resources.

4. **Self-reliance**: Cultivates the habit of seeking information and clarifying doubts independently, which can be a valuable trait in the civil services.

Drawbacks:

1. **Lack of Direction**: Without guidance, there's a risk of getting lost in the vastness of the syllabus or missing out on important topics.

2. **Isolation**: Studying alone might lead to feelings of isolation or lack of motivation, especially when facing challenges.

3. **Lack of Regular Assessment**: Unless self-studying aspirants actively seek out mock tests, they might miss out on regular self-assessment.

Conclusion:

- **Nature of Exam**: CSE is an examination where understanding and analysis are more important than rote memorization. Whether one opts for coaching or self-study, the ability to understand, analyze, and articulate is key.

- **Hybrid Approach**: Many successful candidates use a hybrid approach. They might join coaching for certain tough subjects or for test series while relying on self-study for the rest.

- **Changing Landscape**: With the increasing availability of online resources, many aspirants are opting for online coaching, webinars, and courses, which offer flexibility and the benefits of coaching.

- **Final Word**: Ultimately, the decision between coaching and self-study should be based on an individual's learning style, financial considerations, and personal strengths and weaknesses. There are numerous examples of successful candidates from both categories, which proves that what matters most is dedication, consistency, and an effective strategy.

THE UNIVERSALITY OF THE CSE: UNDERSTANDING ITS ONE-EXAM-FOR-ALL APPROACH AND THE ADVANTAGE OF DIVERSE EDUCATIONAL BACKGROUNDS

The UPSC Civil Services Examination (CSE) in India is often regarded as "one exam for all" due to its comprehensive and inclusive nature. Let's delve into the reasons behind this and understand the implications:

Why is CSE "One Exam for All"?

1. **Unified Civil Services**: The purpose of the CSE is to recruit officers for various services, such as the IAS, IPS, IFS, IRS, and more. A common examination ensures uniformity in the selection process for these different branches of civil services.

2. **Generalist Approach**: The roles that civil servants play require a broad understanding of various subjects and disciplines, rather than a hyper-specialized approach. Hence, the syllabus is designed to test the general awareness, understanding, and analytical skills of the candidates.

3. **Wide Range of Optional Subjects**: While the prelims and general studies papers are designed for a broad audience, the optional papers allow candidates to delve deeper into a specific subject. This system provides a balance between generalist knowledge and specialized understanding.

How does this approach help?

1. **Level Playing Field**: Regardless of one's academic background, everyone is tested on the same set of general studies papers, ensuring that no particular educational background has an undue advantage.

2. **Diversity in Civil Services**: The "one exam for all" approach ensures that the selected candidates come from diverse academic backgrounds. This diversity is essential because civil servants often have to deal with a wide

variety of challenges, and a diverse group brings varied perspectives and solutions to the table.

How do different educational backgrounds help in cracking CSE?

1. **Arts/Humanities**: These graduates are often familiar with subjects like history, geography, political science, and sociology, which form a significant part of the general studies syllabus.

2. **Science/Engineering**: They generally have strong analytical and logical reasoning skills. Subjects like environment and ecology, technology, and data interpretation might be easier for them. Their problem-solving approach can also aid in the case studies section of the ethics paper.

3. **Commerce/Economics**: They have a foundational knowledge of the Indian economy, financial institutions, and economic principles, aiding in the economy section of the general studies papers.

4. **Medical Graduates**: They can leverage their background in the sections on health, biotechnology, and certain aspects of environment and ecology.

5. **Law Graduates**: Their analytical abilities, understanding of the constitution, legal principles, and governance can be beneficial.

Conclusion:

The nature of CSE as "one exam for all" ensures that the selected civil servants are not just knowledgeable in their field of specialization but also have a broad understanding of varied subjects. This holistic education prepares them for the multidimensional challenges they'll face in their roles. Different academic backgrounds bring unique advantages to the table, but it's the ability to integrate, analyze, and present information that plays a pivotal role in cracking the exam.

STRUCTURING SUCCESS: ESSENTIAL ORGANIZING SKILLS FOR CSE ASPIRANTS

Organizing skills are crucial for CSE aspirants given the vastness of the syllabus, the prolonged preparation period, and the multifaceted nature of the examination. Below are some of the critical organizing skills required for CSE aspirants:

1. **Time Management**: Given the vast syllabus, it's imperative for aspirants to manage their time efficiently. This involves setting daily, weekly, and monthly goals, allocating specific times for reading, revision, and practice, and adhering to a strict study routine.

2. **Prioritization**: Not all topics carry the same weight in the examination. Aspirants should be able to prioritize topics based on their importance in the examination, their own strengths and weaknesses, and the time available.

3. **Resource Organization**: Aspirants often have a plethora of study materials – books, notes, online resources, mock tests, etc. Organizing these materials for easy access and systematic study is essential.

4. **Note-making**: The ability to condense vast information into concise, easy-to-revise notes is crucial. Effective note-making helps in quick revisions and ensures that the aspirant remembers key points and concepts.

5. **Planning Revisions**: Given the amount of information to retain, regular revision is a must. Aspirants should have a systematic revision plan to ensure they revisit topics periodically.

6. **Self-assessment**: Organizing regular mock tests and answer-writing sessions helps in gauging one's preparation and understanding which areas need more focus.

7. **Balancing Prelims and Mains Preparation**: While there's a commonality between the two, they require different approaches. Aspirants need to organize their study plan to ensure they're well-prepared for both without neglecting one for the other.

8. **Stress and Health Management**: Organizing breaks, relaxation sessions, physical exercise, and maintaining a balanced diet are crucial. It ensures that aspirants stay mentally and physically fit, which is essential given the stress and rigor of CSE preparation.

9. **Staying Updated**: With current affairs being an integral part of the syllabus, aspirants should have a system to keep themselves updated with the latest events, policies, and developments, and also organize this information for quick revisions.

10. **Feedback Organization**: Aspirants often get feedback from peers, mentors, or coaching institutes. Organizing this feedback, understanding the key areas of improvement, and working on them systematically can greatly enhance preparation quality.

11. **Emotional and Social Management**: It's essential to strike a balance between isolation for studies and social interactions. Organizing occasional meet-ups with fellow aspirants or spending time with family and friends can provide much-needed emotional relief.

In essence, the CSE demands a blend of intellectual prowess and meticulous organization. While knowledge and understanding are vital, the way an aspirant organizes their preparation can be the determining factor in their success. Developing and honing these organizing skills can significantly boost an aspirant's efficiency and effectiveness.

THE MARATHON OF PREPARATION: THE CRUCIAL ROLE OF ENDURANCE AND PERSEVERANCE FOR CSE HOPEFULS

Endurance and perseverance are two of the most crucial qualities for UPSC Civil Services Examination (CSE) aspirants due to the unique nature and challenges of the examination. Here's why:

1. **Long Preparation Phase**: CSE preparation is a marathon, not a sprint. Given the vastness of the syllabus, aspirants often spend one to several years preparing for the exam. Maintaining a consistent study rhythm over such a long duration requires a high degree of endurance.

2. **Vast Syllabus**: The syllabus for the CSE is comprehensive, encompassing diverse topics from ancient history to modern-day international relations, from core sciences to ethics. Persevering through such a wide range of subjects, some of which might be entirely new for the aspirant, is a challenging task.

3. **Uncertainty and Competition**: With a very low selection rate and the dynamic nature of the exam pattern (especially in current affairs and essay papers), there's a significant level of uncertainty. Perseverance becomes vital to keep going despite the odds.

4. **Multiple Stages**: The CSE is divided into three stages: Preliminary, Mains, and the Interview. Each stage has its challenges and requires sustained effort. Even if an aspirant clears the Prelims, they have to muster the energy and determination to prepare intensively for the Mains and subsequently, the Interview.

5. **Physical and Mental Stress**: The long hours of study, the pressure of the looming exams, and the weight of expectations can take a toll on both the body and mind. Endurance is essential to withstand this stress, remain focused, and maintain good health.

6. **Setbacks**: Many aspirants don't succeed in their first attempt. Some face repeated failures. In such situations, perseverance becomes the key to pick oneself up, learn from the mistakes, and keep moving forward.

7. **Balancing Act**: Some aspirants prepare for the CSE while juggling other responsibilities like jobs, postgraduate courses, or family obligations. Endurance is required to manage these multiple fronts effectively.

8. **Continuous Learning**: The nature of CSE demands that aspirants stay updated with current events and continually expand their knowledge base. This continuous learning journey requires both endurance and perseverance.

9. **Changing Dynamics**: Sometimes, even after thorough preparation, the questions can be unpredictable or focus on areas an aspirant might not have concentrated on. Perseverance is required to adapt to such dynamic challenges and not get demotivated.

10. **Emotional Resilience**: There will be moments of doubt, fatigue, and even thoughts of giving up. Perseverance ensures that aspirants navigate through these emotional lows and keep their eyes on the goal.

In conclusion, while intelligence, memory, and analytical skills are undeniably essential for cracking the CSE, it is the blend of endurance and perseverance that carries an aspirant through the highs and lows of the preparation journey. They act as the inner fuel, driving aspirants forward even when the path seems tough.

DECODING THE CSE SYLLABUS: A CRITICAL ASSESSMENT OF PERSPECTIVES, EXPECTATIONS, AND EVALUATION CRITERIA

The Civil Services Examination (CSE) conducted by the Union Public Service Commission (UPSC) in India is renowned for its comprehensive and diverse syllabus. A critical evaluation of its syllabus provides insights into the expectations of the commission, the broader perspectives underlying it, and the rationale for its structure.

1. Perspectives

- **Holistic Development**: The CSE syllabus covers a wide spectrum of topics ranging from history, geography, economy, polity, to current affairs, science and technology, ethics, etc. This broad coverage ensures that a potential civil servant has a well-rounded knowledge base.

- **Interdisciplinary Approach**: Topics are not siloed but are interconnected. For instance, Indian history is not just about dates and events but also about the socio-economic conditions, the impact of colonialism, and the resultant national movement.

- **Analytical and Conceptual Clarity**: The syllabus emphasizes concepts over rote learning. This perspective ensures that aspirants can analyze and interpret any new information or situation.

2. Expectations

- **In-Depth Knowledge**: The commission expects aspirants to delve deep into topics and not just skim the surface. The depth of questions, especially in the Mains examination, indicates this expectation.

- **Current Relevance**: While historical and foundational knowledge is essential, the UPSC also expects candidates to be abreast with contemporary issues and developments.

- **Ethical Grounding**: With a paper dedicated to ethics, integrity, and aptitude, the commission expects future civil servants to be morally upright and ethically sound.

- ◆ **Application of Knowledge**: The ability to apply theoretical knowledge to practical, real-world scenarios is an implicit expectation in the syllabus. This is evident in case studies, problem-solving questions, and the analytical nature of the majority of questions.

3. Evaluations

- ◆ **Pros**:

- ◆ **Comprehensive**: The syllabus ensures a 360-degree understanding of India and the world.

- ◆ **Dynamic**: Incorporates current issues, ensuring that aspirants are up-to-date with recent developments.

- ◆ **Focus on Ethics**: Reinforces the importance of moral integrity in administration.

- ◆ **Cons**:

- ◆ **Vastness**: The sheer breadth can be overwhelming and could favor those who can afford extended periods of study.

- ◆ **Ambiguity**: Some areas of the syllabus are not clearly demarcated, leading to confusion about the depth and breadth of coverage required.

- ◆ **Bias Toward Certain Subjects**: Some argue that there might be undue weightage given to certain topics/subjects at the expense of others in some examination cycles.

Conclusion

The CSE syllabus, with its vastness and depth, aims to select individuals who are not only knowledgeable but also analytical, ethically grounded, and capable of holistic thinking. It reflects the commission's vision of an ideal civil servant – one who is well-versed with the nation's past, engaged with its present, and visionary about its future.

However, it's crucial to remember that no syllabus is perfect. While the CSE syllabus aims to be comprehensive and forward-thinking, criticisms regarding its scope and clarity do hold weight. Continuous feedback and revisions can help ensure that it remains relevant and effective in selecting the best minds for the Indian civil services.

NAVIGATING THE NUANCES: DISTINCTIONS, DIFFERENCES, AND POTENTIAL CONTRADICTIONS AMONG CSE POSTS

The Civil Services Examination (CSE) conducted by the UPSC facilitates recruitment to numerous All India Services and Central Civil Services, each serving distinct roles in the Indian administrative mechanism. While there are inherent differences in the roles and responsibilities associated with each service, they collectively aim to serve the nation's governance structure.

Differences, Distinctions, and Divisions:

1. **All India Services:**

   - **Indian Administrative Service (IAS):** These officers play a vital role in the administration of the states and at the Central level. They are pivotal in policy formulation, implementation, and monitoring.

   - **Indian Police Service (IPS):** IPS officers primarily handle the law and order, crime prevention, and detection aspects in states and at the Central level. They can also serve in central paramilitary forces and intelligence agencies.

   - **Indian Forest Service (IFoS):** Officers in this service manage the nation's forest reserves, wildlife, and the associated ecosystems.

2. **Central Civil Services (Group A and Group B):**

   - **Indian Foreign Service (IFS):** Officers handle India's external affairs, including diplomacy, trade relations, and cultural ties.

   - **Indian Revenue Service (IRS):** They manage taxation, both direct (Income Tax) and indirect (Customs and Central Excise).

   - **Indian Audit and Accounts Service (IA&AS), Indian Civil Accounts Service (ICAS), etc.:** Handle audit, accounts, and financial management aspects of the government.

◆ And many more services such as Indian Railway Traffic Service (IRTS), Indian Information Service (IIS), Indian Defence Estates Service (IDES), etc., each with their specialized roles.

Contradictions or Conflicts:

While the services have clear distinctions in their roles and responsibilities, potential conflicts can arise:

1. **Jurisdictional Overlaps**: Often, particularly in the districts, the IAS (as district magistrate) and the IPS (as superintendent of police) might have different perspectives on a matter, leading to potential conflicts. An administrative decision might have security implications and vice versa.

2. **Priority Differences**: For instance, while an IAS officer might prioritize development works in a region, an IPS officer might be more concerned about the security setup. Similarly, while an IFS officer is concerned with international diplomacy, an IRS officer might prioritize trade revenues.

3. **Resource Allocation**: Resource conflicts can emerge. For instance, decisions on allocating funds can lead to differences in opinions among various services.

4. **Policy Implementation**: Varied interpretations of a policy can sometimes lead to differences in its implementation on the ground.

Conclusion:

While differences and occasional contradictions do exist between various posts filled through the CSE, it's crucial to understand that these distinctions enable the diverse needs of a vast and complex nation to be met efficiently. Coordination mechanisms, periodic training, and inter-service camaraderie often help in resolving such contradictions and ensuring smooth governance. The underlying principle for all these services is the collective aim of public welfare and national development.

ALIGNMENTS AND MISALIGNMENTS: EXAMINING CONFLICTS AMONG CSE CADRES, THEIR ROOTS, AND THE ROLE OF POLITICAL INFLUENCE

The Civil Services Examination (CSE) in India is one of the most challenging examinations, aimed at selecting officers for multiple services, each having distinct roles and responsibilities. Over time, various criticisms have arisen regarding the disparity in roles, powers, and prestige among these services. These issues become particularly pronounced at the field level, where officers from different services often have to collaborate and make collective decisions.

Nature of Conflicts:

1. **Jurisdictional Overlaps**: As officers rise in their careers, roles sometimes overlap. For instance, in a district, both the District Magistrate (usually an IAS officer) and the Superintendent of Police (usually an IPS officer) have significant authority, but their roles can intersect, especially in law and order situations.

2. **Disparity in Power and Prestige**: The IAS, being the premier administrative service, often gets preference in terms of postings, responsibilities, and prominence. This sometimes leads to feelings of resentment among officers of other services.

3. **Varied Training and Perspectives**: Different services have different training modules, which means officers approach problems from varied perspectives. While diversity in perspectives is healthy, it can sometimes lead to disagreements.

Causes of Conflicts:

1. **Hierarchical Structures**: The bureaucratic structure in India is hierarchal. The perceived superiority of one service over another, especially the IAS, has historical roots dating back to the British Raj.

2. **Resource Allocation**: With limited resources, competition can arise regarding allocations, leading to disagreements.

3. **Political Influence**: Local political dynamics can influence decisions at the district level. Politicians might prefer dealing with one officer (or service) over another, leading to power imbalances and conflicts.

Political Influence as a Factor:

1. **Favoritism and Patronage**: Politicians, based on their comfort or the nature of work, might favor officers from a particular service. For instance, for law and order issues, they might lean more towards the IPS, whereas for developmental projects, the IAS might be preferred.

2. **Transfer and Postings**: Political influence in the transfers and postings of officers can sometimes disrupt the harmony among services. A premature transfer of an officer due to political reasons can cause friction among services.

3. **Bypassing Established Norms**: Politicians might sometimes bypass the standard administrative routes to get work done, leading to role conflicts among services.

Critical Evaluation:

While the concerns of disparities among services and political influence are valid, it's essential to understand that the varied services cater to the diverse administrative needs of a vast country. The overlaps, while leading to conflicts, also ensure that no area remains unattended. The key lies in enhancing inter-service camaraderie, ensuring a level playing field in terms of opportunities and postings, and insulating the bureaucracy from undue political interference.

Moreover, with changing times, there's a growing realization about the importance of collaborative governance. Training modules are increasingly focusing on inter-service collaborations, and many officers across services form informal groups to share knowledge and best practices. Such endeavors can significantly reduce conflicts and ensure smoother administration.

STATE CADRE ALLOCATION IN CSE: THE UNDERLYING LOGIC AND ITS IMPLICATIONS FOR CENTRE-STATE RELATIONS

The allotment of cadres (specific states or groups of states) to successful candidates of the Civil Services Examination (CSE) is a systematic process, which has evolved over time to meet the administrative needs of both the states and the center. The procedure seeks to strike a balance between the preferences of the candidates, the needs of different states, and considerations of national integration. Here's a closer look:

Cadre Allocation Policy:

1. **Preferences**: Successful candidates are asked to indicate their cadre preferences in the Detailed Application Form (DAF). They can list all cadres in order of preference.

2. **Home Cadre**: Efforts are made to allot the home cadre (the state from which a candidate hails) to the candidate, but this is subject to availability and certain criteria. For instance, insiders (those who belong to the state) might get preference for the home cadre.

3. **Zonal Preference System**: To make the process more systematic and fair, the cadre allotment system now involves a zonal preference mechanism. Candidates indicate their preferences in terms of zones first, and then in terms of the specific cadres within those zones.

4. **Merit-Cum-Preference**: Cadre allotment is largely based on the rank of the candidate and their preferences. Higher-ranked candidates are more likely to get their top cadre choices.

5. **Service-wise Quota**: There's a fixed number of cadre allotment vacancies for each service (IAS, IPS, IFS, etc.) for each state. Depending on the service a candidate is selected for, the availability of cadres might differ.

6. **Marriage Policy**: If civil servant candidates are married to each other, efforts are made to allocate them the same cadre to avoid administrative hardships arising from living in separate states.

Rationale for State-Center Relations:

1. **National Integration**: One of the primary objectives of sending officers outside their home states is to promote national integration. Officers get to serve in diverse cultural, linguistic, and socio-economic settings, which broadens their perspective.

2. **Neutrality and Objectivity**: An officer serving outside their home state is expected to be more neutral and less influenced by local political dynamics or vested interests.

3. **Cross-fertilization of Ideas**: An officer from one state can bring in best practices and innovative solutions from their native region or from other regions where they have served.

4. **Balanced Development**: By distributing officers from different backgrounds across the country, the idea is to ensure that all regions benefit from a diverse pool of talent and experience.

Conclusion:

While the cadre allocation policy aims to be as systematic and fair as possible, it's not without its critics. Some argue for more localized civil services, while others believe in the merits of a pan-India service. Nonetheless, the existing system seeks to strike a balance between individual preferences and the larger goals of national integration and balanced development.

THE CSE DREAM: WHY IT'S THE PINNACLE OF ASPIRATION FOR INDIAN GRADUATES

The Civil Services Examination (CSE) in India is often viewed as one of the most prestigious exams, and clearing it is considered a significant achievement. The allure of joining the Indian civil services has deep historical, social, and cultural roots. Here's why cracking the CSE is a dream for many graduates in India:

1. **Legacy & Prestige**: The Indian Administrative Service (IAS), Indian Police Service (IPS), Indian Foreign Service (IFS), and other central services have been symbols of prestige, authority, and influence since the colonial era. Being a civil servant, especially an IAS or IPS officer, carries a significant degree of social prestige.

2. **Diverse Role & Impact**: Civil servants have a pivotal role in shaping the future of the country. From policy formulation to grassroots implementation, their decisions impact millions. This power to bring about positive change is a significant motivator.

3. **Job Security**: Unlike many private sector jobs, a career in the civil services offers considerable security. Once inducted, it's rare for civil servants to face abrupt job losses.

4. **Opportunities for Learning**: The vast scope of work in the civil services provides an unparalleled learning experience. Whether it's managing districts, handling law and order situations, or representing India internationally, the exposure is vast.

5. **Diverse Career Paths**: The civil services offer a range of career paths. An IAS officer can work in sectors ranging from education to health to finance, while an IPS officer can delve deep into criminal investigations or cybersecurity. An IFS officer, on the other hand, can represent India in global forums.

6. **Perks & Facilities**: Civil servants enjoy several perks, including government accommodation, official vehicles, and post-retirement benefits. In many regions, they are also given a significant degree of respect by the community.

7. **Challenging Nature of CSE**: The sheer challenge of cracking one of the toughest exams adds to its allure. Clearing the CSE is in itself a testament to one's dedication, intelligence, and hard work.

8. **Cultural & Societal Influence**: In many Indian families and communities, becoming a civil servant is seen as a significant achievement. The societal respect and familial pride associated with it play a substantial role in making it a sought-after career.

9. **Financial Stability**: While the salaries may not be as high as some top private sector jobs, the overall financial stability, combined with perks, makes it an attractive proposition.

10. **Holistic Development**: The training and experiences during service foster a holistic development, instilling leadership qualities, decision-making abilities, and a deep understanding of societal complexities.

Given these factors and the transformative potential of the roles offered through CSE, it's no wonder that many graduates in India aspire to crack the exam and join the revered ranks of the civil services.

The CSE Aspirant's Toolkit: Comprehensive Resources Across Print, Media, and Digital Platforms:

The Civil Services Examination (CSE) in India, conducted by the UPSC, is arguably one of the most challenging competitive exams. Over the years, a plethora of resources has emerged to aid aspirants in their journey. Here's a comprehensive list, broken down by type:

1. **Standard Textbooks (Print):**
   - **History:**
   - "India's Ancient Past" - R.S. Sharma
   - "History of Medieval India" - Satish Chandra
   - "History of Modern India" - Bipan Chandra
   - "India's Struggle for Independence" - Bipan Chandra

- **Polity:**
- "Indian Polity" - M. Laxmikanth
- **Geography:**
- NCERT Class 6-12 Geography textbooks
- "Certificate Physical and Human Geography" - Goh Cheng Leong
- **Economy:**
- "Indian Economy" - Ramesh Singh
- Economic Survey (Published annually by the Ministry of Finance)
- **Environment:**
- "Environment" - Shankar IAS Academy
- **General Science:**
- NCERT Class 6-10 Science textbooks

2. **Current Affairs (Print & Digital):**
   - **Newspapers:**
   - The Hindu
   - Indian Express
   - **Magazines:**
   - Yojana
   - Kurukshetra
   - EPW (Economic and Political Weekly)
   - **Online Portals:**
   - Insights on India
   - Civilsdaily
   - GK Today

3. **Mock Test Series (Digital & Print):**
   - Vajiram and Ravi
   - Vision IAS

- Forum IAS
- Insights on India

4. Online Platforms & E-learning:

- **Websites:**
- Unacademy
- mrunal.org (especially for Economy)
- Byju's
- **YouTube Channels:**
- Rajya Sabha TV (for 'The Big Picture' debates)
- Study IQ
- Let's Crack UPSC CSE (Unacademy's official channel)

5. Coaching Institutes (Traditional Classroom):

- Vajiram and Ravi (New Delhi)
- Rau's IAS (New Delhi)
- Shankar IAS Academy (Chennai)
- ALS IAS (New Delhi)
- Vision IAS (New Delhi)

6. Interview Preparation:

- Mock interviews at coaching institutes like Vajiram, Rau's, and others
- Rajya Sabha TV, Lok Sabha TV for discussion-based programs
- Online portals for current affairs

7. Digital Apps:

- The Hindu official app
- UPSC Pathshala
- Civils Daily app
- Unacademy Learning App

8. **Notes and Material (Digital & Print):**
   - Vision IAS Monthly Current Affairs
   - Insights on India Daily Current Affairs

9. **Miscellaneous:**
   - **Yearbook:**
   - "Manorama Yearbook"
   - "India Yearbook" published by the Publication Division of the Government of India
   - **Reports:**
   - Annual reports of various ministries, especially for Mains examination
   - World Bank, UNDP, and other international organizations' reports as relevant to the syllabus

1. **Standard Textbooks (Print):**
   - **Sociology:**
   - "Sociology: Themes and Perspectives" - Haralambos and Holborn
   - "Indian Society" - Ram Ahuja
   - **International Relations:**
   - "International Relations" - Pavneet Singh
   - "Challenges and Strategies of Indian Foreign Policy" - Rajiv Sikri
   - **Ethics:**
   - "Ethics, Integrity and Aptitude" - G Subba Rao & P N Roy Chowdhury
   - "Lexicon for Ethics, Integrity & Aptitude" - Niraj Kumar
   - **Art and Culture:**
   - "Indian Art and Culture" - Nitin Singhania

2. **Current Affairs (Print & Digital):**
   - Newspapers:
   - The Times of India

- The Telegraph
- **Online Portals:**
- IASbaba
- Drishti IAS

3. **Mock Test Series (Digital & Print):**
   - KSG India
   - IASbaba's TLP (Think, Learn & Perform)

4. **Online Platforms & E-learning:**
   - **Websites:**
   - ClearIAS
   - IAS Score
   - **YouTube Channels:**
   - Drishti IAS
   - Prashant Dhawan's channel for Environment and Geography

5. **Coaching Institutes (Traditional Classroom):**
   - Chanakya IAS Academy
   - KSG India
   - Drishti IAS

6. **Digital Apps:**
   - IASbaba
   - ClearIAS
   - Daily Current Affairs UPSC IAS

7. **Miscellaneous:**
   - **NCERTs:**
   - All NCERTs, especially from Class 6-12, are vital, including subjects like Economics, Political Science, and Ancient & Medieval India.
   - **Group Study:**

- Collaborating with fellow aspirants to share knowledge and discuss various topics. This aids in diverse perspective understanding and keeping up motivation levels.
- **Answer Writing Practice Platforms:**
- Secure Initiative by Insights on India
- TLP by IASbaba

8. **Subject-specific websites and portals:**
   - **Geography & Environment:**
   - Down To Earth website
   - Environics Trust
   - **Economics:**
   - Arthapedia
   - RBI's official website for reports and data
   - **Polity & Governance:**
   - PRS India for legislative updates
   - IDSA for security and defense-related articles

1. **Standard Textbooks (Print & Digital):**
   - **Public Administration:**
   - "Public Administration" - M. Laxmikanth
   - "New Horizons of Public Administration" - Mohit Bhattacharya
   - **Anthropology:**
   - "Anthropology Simplified" - Vivek Bhasme
   - **Economics:**
   - "Indian Economy" - Uma Kapila

2. **Current Affairs (Digital):**
   - **Online Portals:**
   - OnlyIAS

+ AffairsCloud for quick updates

+ The Better India (for positive stories, often asked in interviews)

3. **Mock Test Series (Digital & Print):**

+ GS Score

+ Next IAS

+ Anudeep Durishetty's blog (AIR 1, 2017) for answer writing strategies and book recommendations

4. **Online Platforms & E-learning:**

+ **Websites:**

+ NeoStencil

+ Oliveboard for mock tests and quizzes

+ **YouTube Channels:**

+ NeoStencil

+ Let's Study Together

+ Sleepy Classes

5. **Coaching Institutes (Traditional Classroom & Online):**

+ IAS Gurukul

+ The Prayas India (Mumbai-based)

+ Ensemble IAS Academy

+ O2 IAS Academy

+ **Online Platforms:**

+ Khan GS Research Center (popular for its approach in General Studies)

+ Flavido for online notes and materials

6. **Research Platforms:**

+ **EPWRF (Economic and Political Weekly Research Foundation):** Provides a variety of economic and financial data on India.

- **ORF (Observer Research Foundation)**: Great for articles and research on International Relations, Security Issues, and more.

- **CPR (Centre for Policy Research)**: Covers a wide range of topics including governance, urbanization, etc.

7. Digital Apps:

- Gradeup: Offers quizzes, mock tests, and daily current affairs.

- PIB (Press Information Bureau) app: Official updates from the Government of India.

- RSTV app: For programs like "The Big Picture" and "India's World".

8. Miscellaneous Online Resources:

- **Quiz Platforms:**

- JetPunk or Sporcle for geography and world affairs quizzes.

- PrelimsMCQ for daily MCQs based on current affairs.

9. Subject-specific websites and portals:

- **Law:**

- LiveLaw and Bar & Bench: For updates on important judgments, legal news.

- **Environment:**

- Mongabay India: News and features on environment issues.

- **Science and Technology:**

- ISRO's official website: For space and tech updates.

- DST (Department of Science and Technology) website: For research updates and S&T policies.

1. Websites for Comprehensive Coverage:

- **Civilsdaily:** It's known for its daily news capsules, and its unique "story" format helps connect current events with static topics.

- **GKToday:** It offers both current affairs and general knowledge materials, especially beneficial for prelims.

- **BYJU's IAS:** They provide free current affairs magazines monthly which are concise and relevant.

2. **Online Platforms & E-learning:**

   - **Mrunal.org:** Particularly good for Economics, Geography, and Environment topics. Mrunal's video lectures are quite popular among aspirants.

   - **Unacademy:** It's a platform where many educators provide courses on various subjects. The user reviews can help pinpoint the best ones.

3. **YouTube Channels:**

   - **StudyIQ Education:** Covers a broad range of topics related to UPSC syllabus.

   - **UPSC Pathshala:** Provides topic-wise detailed videos.

   - **BYJU'S IAS:** Apart from their website, their YouTube channel is also full of valuable lectures and current affairs discussions.

4. **Mock Test Platforms:**

   - **Vision IAS:** Known for its test series and detailed explanation for each question.

   - **Insights on India:** Their daily current affairs quiz is quite popular.

5. **Digital Libraries and Databases:**

   - **Shodhganga:** A reservoir of theses from Indian researchers. Useful for obtaining in-depth research materials.

   - **JSTOR:** Provides access to thousands of academic journal articles, books, and primary sources.

6. **Miscellaneous Digital Resources:**

   - **Yojana and Kurukshetra magazines:** Both are published by the Govt of India. Yojana provides in-depth analysis on a particular topic every month.

   - **Rajya Sabha TV programs:** Shows like 'The Big Picture' provide in-depth analysis of current affairs.

7. Coaching Institutes:

- **Rau's IAS:** Renowned for its general studies program.

- **ALS IAS:** It has produced numerous toppers in the past.

8. Telegram Groups:

- Many educators and online portals have their own Telegram groups where they share study materials, quizzes, and news summaries.

9. Additional Research Websites:

- **Brookings India:** For policy research, especially economics and international relations.

- **IDFC Institute:** Research in the areas of political economy, development, and governance.

10. Bookstores and Publishers:

- **Rajiv Beri's Bahri Sons in Khan Market, Delhi:** Known for its collection of UPSC related books.

- **Mains 365 by Vision IAS:** This series covers current affairs for mains examination topic-wise.

1. Websites for Comprehensive Coverage:

- **IASbaba:** Offers daily news analysis, current affairs, and a very popular initiative called "60 Day Plan" for preliminary exam revision.

- **IDSA (Institute for Defence Studies and Analyses):** Great resource for international relations and defense-related topics.

2. YouTube Channels:

- **Drishti IAS:** Their explanations in Hindi and English are quite thorough.

- **Learners' Planet:** Offers videos on various topics especially helpful for Science and Technology.

- **IAS Academy:** Offers a plethora of tutorials ranging from current affairs to subject-specific concepts.

3. Podcasts:

- **Bharatvaarta:** Covers policy, politics, culture, and history.

- ◆ **Pulse by Unacademy:** Addresses current affairs topics with subject matter experts.

4. **Mock Test Platforms:**
   - ◆ **IASbaba's TLP (Think, Learn & Perform):** Their mains answer writing initiative is beneficial for practice.
   - ◆ **ForumIAS:** They offer test series and also have a '9 PM brief' which summarizes daily current affairs.

5. **Digital Apps:**
   - ◆ **ClearIAS:** Offers notes, mock tests, and current affairs.
   - ◆ **IASbaba's mobile app:** Provides daily current affairs, quizzes, and the "60 Day Plan".

6. **Coaching Institutes:**
   - ◆ **Shankar IAS Academy:** Famous especially for their Environment and Ecology notes.
   - ◆ **KSG (Khan Study Group):** Has produced several toppers and is known for its mains test series.

7. **Blogs of Previous Year Toppers:**
   - ◆ **Anudeep Durishetty's Blog:** (AIR 1, 2017) provides detailed strategies, booklists, and answer sheets.
   - ◆ **Gaurav Agrawal's Blog:** (AIR 1, 2013) includes his detailed notes on various subjects.

8. **Other Books and Publications:**
   - ◆ **Quarterly Current Affairs - Disha Publications:** Good for a quick revision of past months' happenings.
   - ◆ **India Year Book:** Published by the Publication Division, it's an authentic compilation of complete information about India's current affairs.

9. **Online Q&A Forums:**
   - ◆ **Quora:** There are dedicated spaces and many UPSC toppers who answer queries related to preparation strategies, booklists, etc.

10. Other Digital Resources:

- **PIB's YouTube channel:** Offers official videos of government events, press conferences, etc.

- **Evernote:** A note-taking app beneficial for making and organizing notes.

11. Regional News Websites:

- For a more regional perspective on issues (important for both GS and optional papers like Anthropology or Sociology), websites of regional newspapers or portals like **The News Minute (for South India)** can be beneficial.

This list is comprehensive but not exhaustive. The CSE syllabus is vast, and hence there are various sources for different topics. The key is not to gather many resources but to thoroughly study selected ones.

While these resources are valuable, it's essential to remember that relying on too many can become overwhelming. It's often better to choose high-quality resources and study them in-depth rather than skimming through a vast number of materials.

As previously mentioned, while there are numerous resources available, the trick lies in choosing a few and sticking to them. Constantly jumping between resources can become counterproductive. It's essential to find a balance between breadth (covering a vast syllabus) and depth (understanding concepts thoroughly).

MASTERING THE CSE: PROVEN STRATEGIES FOR ASPIRANTS TO ACHIEVE SUCCESS

Cracking the UPSC Civil Services Examination (CSE) requires a combination of the right study materials, a well-thought-out plan, consistent hard work, and mental fortitude. Here's a holistic strategy to consider for CSE aspirants:

1. **Understand the Syllabus:**
   - The CSE syllabus is vast but defined. Get thoroughly acquainted with the syllabus for both the Preliminary and Mains examination. Know which topics need a deep dive and which ones need a broader overview.

2. **Integrate Current Affairs:**
   - Read a standard newspaper daily, like *The Hindu* or *Indian Express*. Make concise notes, connecting the news with the static syllabus.

3. **Choose the Right Resources:**
   - Limit your resources to avoid information overload. It's better to revise one book multiple times than to read multiple books once.

4. **Time Management:**
   - Break your preparation into smaller, manageable goals, like completing a specific subject or topic within a set time frame. Stick to a daily routine.
   - Allocate time separately for Prelims and Mains preparation but ensure that they are not mutually exclusive.

5. **Answer Writing Practice for Mains:**
   - Start practicing answer writing early on. This helps in internalizing information, improves recall, and makes you exam-ready.
   - Enroll in a test series or practice with past year papers.

6. Mock Tests for Prelims:

- Regularly solve mock tests to assess your preparation level, improve speed, and reduce errors.

- Analyze each test to identify weak areas.

7. Selecting the Optional Subject:

- Choose an optional subject based on your interest, availability of study material, and previous years' question trends. Remember, an interest in the subject can be a game-changer during stressful times.

8. Stay Updated with UPSC's Notifications:

- Keep an eye on the official UPSC website for any notifications or changes in the pattern, dates, or syllabus.

9. Group Study (Optional):

- Group discussions can be beneficial to gain different perspectives on a topic. However, ensure that group studies are productive.

10. Revision:

- The human brain tends to forget; hence, revision is crucial. Make short notes or flashcards for quick revisions.

11. Stay Physically and Mentally Fit:

- Incorporate some physical activity into your daily routine. Meditation and mindfulness practices can help maintain focus and reduce stress.

12. Avoid Negative Influences:

- Stay away from naysayers or any sources of negativity. Surround yourself with positivity, perhaps with fellow aspirants who are serious about their goals.

13. Continue Evolving:

- If a strategy doesn't seem to be working after giving it a fair shot, don't be afraid to tweak it or change it. What works for one person might not work for another.

14. Stay Persistent:

- CSE is as much a test of one's perseverance as it is of one's knowledge. There might be times when you feel down or demotivated, but remember why you started.

Lastly, while it's essential to be dedicated to your preparation, it's also crucial to maintain a balance. Take regular breaks, spend time with loved ones, and engage in hobbies or activities that relax you. Remember, it's a marathon, not a sprint.

DECIPHERING THE CSE BLUEPRINT: EFFECTIVE TECHNIQUES FOR ASPIRANTS TO GRASP THE SYLLABUS

Understanding the UPSC Civil Services Examination (CSE) syllabus is pivotal to your preparation. Here are some techniques and strategies to deeply and effectively understand the syllabus:

1. **Break It Down:**

    ◆ Start by getting a printout of the official syllabus from the UPSC website.

    ◆ Divide the syllabus into broad subjects and then further into topics and subtopics. This will give you a hierarchical structure to work with.

2. **Relate to Current Affairs:**

    ◆ As you go through each topic, try to relate it with current events. This helps in integrating static knowledge with dynamic current affairs, which is crucial for the CSE.

3. **Mind Maps:**

    ◆ Create mind maps for each subject. This graphical way of representing topics and subtopics can make understanding and revision more effective.

4. **Highlight Keywords:**

    ◆ In each topic or subtopic, underline or highlight keywords. For instance, in a topic like "Indian freedom struggle," words like "moderate phase," "extremist phase," "Quit India Movement" are key points.

5. **Regular Revision:**

    ◆ The syllabus is vast, and you may forget some parts if you don't revisit them. Schedule regular revision cycles.

6. Use the Syllabus Actively:

- Every time you study a topic or read a book, always have the syllabus next to you. This will help you stay aligned with what UPSC expects you to know.

- When reading newspapers or current affairs, having the syllabus handy can help you pick out relevant news articles.

7. Create Personal Notes:

- Make succinct notes for each topic and subtopic. Use flowcharts, diagrams, and bullets. These notes will be your go-to for quick revisions.

8. Mock Tests and Previous Year Questions:

- Regularly attempt mock tests and solve previous year's questions related to each topic. This will give you a practical understanding of how topics from the syllabus are converted into questions.

9. Engage in Discussions:

- Discuss the syllabus with fellow aspirants. This not only solidifies your understanding but also gives you insights into parts of the syllabus you might have overlooked.

10. Online Resources:

- Use online platforms like YouTube, where many educators break down and explain the syllabus. However, always cross-reference to ensure accuracy.

11. Teaching:

- A unique way to understand something is to teach it. Explain parts of the syllabus to friends, family, or even fellow aspirants. As you articulate, you'll find gaps in your understanding, which you can then address.

12. Stay Updated:

- UPSC occasionally revises the syllabus. Stay updated by regularly checking the official UPSC website.

Understanding the CSE syllabus isn't just about reading it a few times. It's about internalizing it, making it a part of your study routine, and consistently relating what you learn to the topics and subtopics. It acts as a lighthouse, ensuring that your preparation is always on the right path.

MERGING NEWS WITH NOTES: STRATEGIES FOR CSE ASPIRANTS TO SEAMLESSLY INTEGRATE CURRENT AFFAIRS INTO THEIR PREPARATION

Integrating current affairs into the preparation for the UPSC Civil Services Examination (CSE) is of paramount importance, given the dynamic nature of the exam. Here's a systematic approach to seamlessly weave current affairs into your studies:

1. **Start with a Reliable Newspaper:**
   - Dedicate time daily to read a reputed newspaper such as *The Hindu*, *Indian Express*, or *The Times of India*. This is essential for both Prelims and Mains. Focus more on national, international, and editorial pages.

2. **Relate News with the Syllabus:**
   - While reading, continuously relate the news articles to the static topics in your UPSC syllabus. This will help in linking current happenings with basic concepts.

3. **Make Notes:**
   - Create daily/weekly notes. Write concise points, noting down the key facts, figures, and arguments. Over time, this will become an invaluable revision tool.

4. **Refer to a Monthly Magazine or Digest:**
   - A number of institutions and websites release monthly current affairs magazines or digests, especially tailored for UPSC. These can help consolidate your understanding.

5. **Use the Internet:**
   - Websites, blogs, and forums like *Insights on India*, *IASbaba*, and *Civilsdaily* offer daily current affairs summaries, quizzes, and discussions.

6. Government Websites and Publications:

- Websites of ministries, PIB (Press Information Bureau), PRS Legislative, etc., provide official data, policies, bills, and other relevant updates.

7. Focus on Issues, Not Just Events:

- Rather than just noting down events, understand the underlying issues. For instance, if there's news about a new environmental policy, understand its implications, the problems it seeks to address, international comparisons, and potential challenges.

8. Use Current Affairs for Answer Writing:

- When practicing answer writing for Mains, incorporate current affairs, data, examples, and case studies from your daily readings. This enriches your answers and makes them stand out.

9. Discussion Groups:

- Engage in group discussions with fellow aspirants. It exposes you to different perspectives on current issues.

10. Special Focus on Editorials and Opinions:

- The editorial and opinion sections of newspapers provide in-depth analysis, pros, cons, and criticisms of current issues. They help in understanding the nuances and forming a balanced view.

11. Stay Updated with International News:

- Follow international news portals or watch programs like BBC World News to get a broader perspective on global events and India's role.

12. Regularly Attempt Current Affairs Quizzes:

- Online platforms offer daily and weekly current affairs quizzes. These help in retaining information and gauging your understanding.

13. Audio and Video Resources:

- Platforms like YouTube have many channels dedicated to current affairs discussions, like Rajya Sabha TV's "The Big Picture". These can aid auditory learners.

14. Revise Regularly:

- The vastness of current affairs mandates regular revision. Revisit your notes and magazines periodically.

15. Stay Away from Sensational News:

- Avoid sensationalist or trivial news. UPSC focuses on issues of national and international importance, not on controversies or scandals.

Remember, integrating current affairs isn't just about knowing the latest happenings. It's about understanding their context, relevance, and implications in the larger framework of the nation and the world.

CHARTING THE PATH TO CSE SUCCESS: SELECTING THE IDEAL RESOURCES, LOCATING THEM, AND EVALUATING THE INVESTMENT

Choosing the right resources is critical for UPSC Civil Services Examination (CSE) preparation. The right materials can make a vast difference in understanding and retention. Here's a guide to help CSE aspirants choose wisely:

1. **Start with the Syllabus and Previous Years' Papers:**

   ◆ Before purchasing any material, familiarize yourself with the UPSC syllabus and go through the last 5-10 years' question papers. This gives an idea about the areas to focus on.

2. **Basic Books:**

   ◆ Begin with standard NCERT textbooks, especially for history, geography, economy, and polity. They offer a solid foundation.

   ◆ For advanced reading, books like *Laxmikanth* for Polity, *Ramesh Singh* for Economy, and *Spectrum* for Modern India are popular choices.

3. **Current Affairs:**

   ◆ A daily reading of a reputed national newspaper (like *The Hindu* or *Indian Express*) is crucial. The yearly subscription could be around INR 2000-2500.

   ◆ Monthly magazines tailored for UPSC like *Yojana*, *Kurukshetra*, and others can be beneficial. Each issue might cost between INR 30-50.

4. **Online Portals and Apps:**

   ◆ Websites like *Insights on India*, *IASbaba*, and *Civilsdaily* offer daily current affairs, notes, and mock tests. Some content is free, while comprehensive courses might cost from INR 10,000 to INR 50,000 depending on the depth and duration of the course.

- There are mobile applications such as UPSC Pathshala, ClearIAS, etc., which have both free resources and paid courses.

5. Coaching Institutes:

- Although not mandatory, many aspirants opt for coaching. Fees for full courses in renowned institutes range from INR 1,00,000 to INR 2,50,000 or more. It's essential to do thorough research, check reviews, and perhaps attend a few demo classes before enrolling.

6. Mock Tests and Test Series:

- Regularly attempting mock tests is essential. Various institutes and websites offer test series. The cost varies but might be around INR 5,000 to INR 15,000 for a comprehensive series.

7. Optional Subject Materials:

- Depending on the optional you choose, you'll need specialized books or coaching. For instance, if you select Anthropology, you might refer to *Ember and Ember*. The cost for optional subject materials can range from INR 2,000 to INR 10,000 or more.

8. Libraries and Study Centers:

- Instead of purchasing every book, you can join libraries or use reading rooms available in coaching hubs like Delhi's Mukherjee Nagar or Rajinder Nagar. Membership fees vary but could be around INR 500 to INR 3,000 a year.

Guidelines for Choosing the Right Resources:

- **Avoid Piling Up Too Many Books:** Quality over quantity. More books can lead to confusion.

- **Recommendations:** Talk to seniors or those who've cleared the exam for their advice on materials.

- **Review and Cross-Check:** Before purchasing any material, especially online courses, check reviews and ratings.

♦ **Stay Updated:** UPSC's pattern and focus areas can evolve. Ensure that your materials are the latest editions.

Remember, the cost is variable. While some candidates might spend a significant amount, others have cleared the UPSC CSE with minimal expenditure, relying on self-study, free online resources, and libraries. It's more about how you use the resources than how many you have.

1. Interactive Learning Platforms:

♦ **Unacademy:** A popular online platform that provides both free lessons and paid courses. The subscription cost varies based on duration. For example, a 12-month subscription might cost around INR 40,000. The platform often provides discounts, so prices can vary.

♦ **Byju's:** Offers comprehensive IAS preparation modules. Packages range from INR 50,000 to INR 70,000.

Time & Place: As these are online platforms, you can learn anytime, anywhere.

2. Optional Subject Coaching:

♦ Depending on the city and the subject, coaching can cost between INR 30,000 to INR 50,000. For instance, Maths optional in Delhi might cost more due to the subject's complexity and demand.

Time & Place: Typically, these courses are 3-6 months long and are available in major cities like Delhi, Bangalore, and Hyderabad.

3. Study Material Packages:

♦ Some institutes and websites offer comprehensive study materials, which can be a mix of books, magazines, and online resources. The cost might range from INR 10,000 to INR 20,000.

Time & Place: Delivered to your doorstep or available for pickup at coaching centers.

4. Prelims and Mains Exclusive Test Series:

♦ There are exclusive test series for both stages of the exam. They might cost anywhere from INR 5,000 to INR 15,000 based on the institute's reputation and depth of the series.

Time & Place: Both offline in cities like Delhi and online.

5. Interview Guidance Programs:

- After clearing the Mains, some candidates opt for mock interview sessions. The cost can range from INR 2,000 to INR 10,000 based on the institute and the number of mock interviews.

Time & Place: Usually in cities like Delhi where retired bureaucrats and experts provide guidance.

6. Study Groups and Discussion Forums:

- While this doesn't have a direct cost, traveling to meet with study groups or attending seminars can have associated costs.

Time & Place: Can be organized in local libraries, universities, or online platforms like Telegram and Zoom.

7. Renting a Room in Study Hubs:

- Places like Mukherjee Nagar in Delhi are popular study hubs where aspirants rent rooms. Monthly rent can vary from INR 5,000 to INR 15,000 or more depending on the facilities.

Time: As long as the preparation phase. **Place:** Areas in Delhi, Bangalore, Pune, Hyderabad, etc.

8. Workshops and Seminars:

- Occasionally, workshops or seminars by experts are conducted. They might be free or can have a fee ranging from INR 500 to INR 5,000 based on the expert's reputation and the duration.

Time & Place: Major cities, and sometimes online. Duration can be a day to a week.

Remember, while these are approximate costs, they can vary based on the quality, demand, and changes in the market. Always cross-check the latest prices and reviews before making a commitment.

MASTERING THE CLOCK: THE IMPORTANCE OF TIME MANAGEMENT AND EFFECTIVE STRATEGIES FOR CSE ASPIRANTS

Time management is pivotal for a Civil Services Examination (CSE) aspirant. Given the vastness of the syllabus, the uncertainty surrounding the nature of questions, and the high level of competition, ensuring every minute is used productively becomes paramount. Here's why time management is vital and how it can be used effectively:

Importance of Time Management for CSE Aspirants:

1. **Vast Syllabus:** The UPSC syllabus is exhaustive. Efficient time management ensures that every topic gets its due attention without spending excess time on just one section.

2. **Balance Prelims and Mains:** While both stages have overlapping syllabi, the method of answering differs. Managing time ensures a balanced preparation for both.

3. **Optional Subject:** The optional subject needs special attention, as it can be a scoring area. Time management helps in providing adequate time for its preparation.

4. **Regular Revision:** Just reading is not enough. Regular revision ensures retention, and managing time will help allot hours for revision.

5. **Current Affairs:** This isn't a one-time read. Newspapers, monthly magazines, and updates demand daily attention.

6. **Practice:** Writing answers, solving MCQs, and mock tests need scheduled time. They offer real exam-time experience and are as crucial as studying.

7. **Personal Well-being:** Continuous study can lead to burnout. Managed breaks, relaxation, and recreation are crucial for mental well-being.

Effective Time Management Techniques:

1. **Set Clear Goals:** Define what you wish to achieve daily, weekly, and monthly. For example, set a target for finishing a particular topic or subject.

2. **Prioritize Tasks:** Not all subjects or topics carry the same weight. Recognize priority areas and allocate more time to them.

3. **Make a Study Schedule:** Stick to a daily routine. Allocate fixed hours for general studies, optional subjects, current affairs, and practice tests.

4. **Avoid Multitasking:** Contrary to popular belief, multitasking can reduce your efficiency. Focus on one topic at a time.

5. **Use Techniques like Pomodoro:** Study for 25 minutes and then take a 5-minute break. This keeps the mind fresh and increases productivity.

6. **Limit Distractions:** Keep mobile phones, social media, and other distractions at bay during study hours.

7. **Allocate Time for Revision:** As you progress, ensure you allocate time for revising already studied topics.

8. **Self-assess Regularly:** Give mock tests to gauge your preparation level and adjust your schedule based on the results.

9. **Stay Flexible:** While a routine is good, be prepared to modify your schedule based on unexpected events or if you feel certain areas need more attention.

10. **Health and Recreation:** Allocate time for physical exercise, meditation, or any form of recreation. It helps in refreshing the mind.

In essence, effective time management is about creating a balance. It ensures comprehensive coverage of the syllabus, repeated revisions, and consistent practice, while also keeping the aspirant's mental health in check. For an exam as demanding as the UPSC CSE, managing one's time efficiently can very well be the difference between success and disappointment.

THE POMODORO TECHNIQUE: A COMPARATIVE ANALYSIS OF ITS BENEFITS FOR CSE ASPIRANTS AGAINST OTHER TIME-MANAGEMENT METHODS

The **Pomodoro Technique** is a time management method developed by Francesco Cirillo in the late 1980s. The technique breaks work into intervals, traditionally 25 minutes long, separated by short breaks, usually five minutes. These intervals are termed "pomodoros", the plural in English of the Italian word pomodoro (tomato), after the tomato-shaped kitchen timer that Cirillo used as a university student.

Here's a basic breakdown of the Pomodoro Technique:

1. **Choose a Task:** Decide on the task you want to work on.

2. **Set the Timer:** Traditionally, this is set to 25 minutes.

3. **Work on the Task:** Immerse yourself in the task for the set duration, and try to avoid all interruptions.

4. **End Work When the Timer Rings:** Put a checkmark on a piece of paper to record your completed session.

5. **Take a Short Break:** After one pomodoro, take a 5-minute break.

6. **Repeat:** After completing four pomodoros, take a longer break of 15-30 minutes.

Benefits of Pomodoro for CSE Aspirants:

1. **Enhances Focus:** The structured intervals help aspirants stay focused on a specific topic without being overwhelmed by the vast syllabus.

2. **Prevents Burnout:** Regular breaks ensure that the brain does not get fatigued.

3. **Provides Structure:** Helps in planning and organizing study sessions better.

4. **Encourages Consistent Revision:** The regular intervals can also be used to revisit and revise previously covered content.

5. **Enhances Productivity:** With the pressure of a timer, aspirants might find themselves working more efficiently.

Comparison with Other Techniques:

1. **Marathon Study Sessions:** Unlike Pomodoro's short bursts, marathon sessions involve extended periods of studying without breaks. While it might seem like a more extended session means more content coverage, it often leads to quicker burnout and less retention.

2. **Task-based Study:** Instead of time-based targets as in Pomodoro, students set task-based targets (e.g., completing a chapter). While this ensures task completion, it doesn't offer the flexibility of the Pomodoro technique. A challenging topic could take hours without a structured break, leading to fatigue.

3. **Interval Studying without Set Times:** Similar to Pomodoro, but without strict timing. Students take breaks when they feel like it. While this offers flexibility, it doesn't have the structured efficiency of the Pomodoro method.

For **CSE aspirants**, the vastness and depth of the syllabus can become overwhelming. The Pomodoro Technique offers an organized approach, ensuring that students not only cover topics but also retain them, all while maintaining their mental well-being. That said, every individual is unique, and while Pomodoro might work wonders for some, others might find different techniques more suitable. It's essential to understand one's learning style and choose a method accordingly.

PENNING THE PERFECT RESPONSE: THE CRUCIAL ROLE AND IMPACT OF ANSWER WRITING PRACTICE FOR CSE MAINS ASPIRANTS

Answer writing practice for the UPSC Civil Services Mains examination is one of the most emphasized areas of preparation, and rightly so. The Mains exam is highly descriptive and demands a unique combination of analytical ability, presentation skills, and content knowledge. Here's why answer writing practice is crucial for CSE aspirants:

1. **Content Structuring:** While aspirants might have vast knowledge about a topic, presenting it within the limited time and word count is challenging. Regular answer writing helps in structuring the answer with an introduction, body, and conclusion in an efficient and impactful manner.

2. **Time Management:** Each question in the Mains examination has to be answered in a stipulated time to complete the paper. Regular practice helps aspirants gauge how much time they should ideally spend on each answer.

3. **Improved Presentation:** How one presents an answer can make a significant difference. Using diagrams, flowcharts, and underlining important points can fetch more marks. Practice helps in refining this skill.

4. **Addressing the Demand of the Question:** UPSC questions are often twisted and demand a specific answer. They might not be direct queries. With practice, aspirants learn to understand what exactly the question is asking and tailor their answers accordingly.

5. **Enhanced Analytical Abilities:** UPSC doesn't just test knowledge. It tests the ability to analyze, correlate, and present arguments. Answer writing hones these analytical abilities.

6. **Feedback Loop:** Regular answer writing, especially in test series or under a mentor, allows aspirants to get feedback. This feedback is crucial to understand where one is lacking and how one can improve.

7. **Building Stamina:** Writing for hours during the actual Mains examination can be physically exhausting. Regular practice builds stamina and ensures that aspirants don't feel fatigued during the real exam.

8. **Boosting Confidence:** Going into the examination with ample answer writing practice boosts confidence. Aspirants feel better prepared to tackle a variety of questions.

9. **Reducing Silly Mistakes:** With consistent practice, aspirants can identify and rectify recurring mistakes, whether they're conceptual errors, presentation flaws, or grammatical mistakes.

10. **Knowledge Reinforcement:** Writing answers reinforces knowledge. It's an active form of learning and helps in better retention compared to passive reading.

The influence of answer writing practice is evident in the results. Aspirants who regularly practice, refine, and innovate in their answer writing style tend to score better in the Mains, which is a significant portion of the total marks in the UPSC Civil Services Examination. Given the intense competition, even a few marks can make a significant difference in the rank and, subsequently, the service and cadre allocation.

TACKLING THE CSE PRELIMS: THE INDISPENSABLE ROLE OF MOCK TESTS IN ACHIEVING SUCCESS

Mock tests play a vital role in the preparation of UPSC Civil Services Preliminary Examination. The preliminary examination is the first and most critical hurdle aspirants need to cross to progress to the Mains stage. Here's how mock tests can be immensely beneficial for Prelims:

1. **Understanding the Exam Pattern:** Mock tests help aspirants get a feel of the actual examination pattern. They get acquainted with the type of questions asked, the varying difficulty levels, and the distribution of questions among different subjects.

2. **Time Management:** The Prelims paper, especially the General Studies (GS) paper, requires answering a large number of questions in a limited time frame. Mock tests help aspirants strategize about how to allocate time effectively.

3. **Identification of Weak Areas:** By regularly attempting mock tests, aspirants can identify subjects or topics they are weak in. This helps in focused revision and plugging knowledge gaps.

4. **Accuracy and Elimination Techniques:** The negative marking in the Prelims exam means that blind guessing can be harmful. Mock tests teach aspirants to enhance their accuracy and use intelligent elimination techniques to tackle tricky questions.

5. **Building Stamina:** Sitting for long hours and maintaining concentration can be a challenge. Regularly attempting full-length mock tests conditions the mind and body for the actual examination day.

6. **Boosting Confidence:** Scoring well in mock tests can be a morale booster. Conversely, if an aspirant doesn't perform well, it serves as a wake-up call, indicating that more preparation is needed.

7. **Adapting to Various Question Types:** UPSC is known to throw surprises. Over a series of mock tests, aspirants get exposed to a wide variety of

questions which prepares them for any unexpected twists in the actual exam.

8. **Revision:** Mock tests often cover a vast portion of the syllabus. Every test taken is a revision of multiple topics, reinforcing knowledge and aiding retention.

9. **Performance Analysis:** Many coaching institutes provide a detailed analysis of mock test performances, benchmarking an aspirant's performance against peers. This can be a valuable tool to understand where one stands in the competition.

10. **Stress Management:** By simulating actual exam conditions, mock tests help in reducing anxiety and stress. When aspirants sit for the real exam, they feel like they are just taking another mock test.

Given the intensely competitive nature of the UPSC Prelims, where even a single mark can make the difference between progressing to the Mains or being eliminated, mock tests are not just advisable but essential. Regular practice through mock tests, followed by an honest assessment and corrective action, maximizes an aspirant's chances of clearing the Preliminary Examination.

Navigating the Choice: Optimal Strategies for Selecting the Optional Subject in CSE. Top of Form

Selecting the optional subject for the UPSC Civil Services Examination is a significant decision for every aspirant, as it can make or break their chances of success. The optional subject carries a substantial weightage in the Mains examination. Here are some strategies to consider when choosing the optional subject:

1. **Interest and Passion:** Choose a subject you are genuinely interested in. You will spend many hours reading, understanding, and writing about this subject, so it's crucial that it holds your attention and doesn't become monotonous.

2. **Background Knowledge:** Consider your academic background. If the optional subject aligns with what you've studied previously, it can be advantageous as you'd already have a foundational understanding.

3. **Availability of Study Material:** Some subjects have abundant resources, coaching facilities, and guidance available, both online and

offline. Ensure that you have access to comprehensive and quality material for the subject you choose.

4. **Syllabus Overlap:** Subjects that have a significant overlap with the General Studies papers can be beneficial. For instance, subjects like Geography, Political Science, and Public Administration have portions that coincide with the GS papers, which can reduce the overall preparation load.

5. **Past Trends:** While it's not advisable to rely solely on this, looking at the past years' question papers and toppers' choices can give an insight into the nature of questions asked and the scoring pattern of a particular subject.

6. **Manageability of Syllabus:** Some optional subjects have vast syllabuses, while others are more concise. Ensure that you can cover and revise the syllabus multiple times before the examination.

7. **Guidance and Mentoring:** If you have access to a mentor or teacher specializing in a particular optional subject, it might tilt the scales in favor of that subject.

8. **Scoring Potential:** Some subjects are perceived as more 'scoring' than others. While this shouldn't be the sole criterion, it's worth considering if you're torn between two or more subjects.

9. **Check Success Ratio:** Analyze the success ratio of candidates who chose a particular optional. While this is a dynamic metric and changes year-on-year, it can provide a general idea.

10. **Self-assessment:** Take a week or more to study a few topics from the subjects you are considering. This self-assessment will give you a feel for the subject, and you can gauge how comfortable you are with its content and depth.

11. **Avoid Herd Mentality:** Just because many candidates are opting for a particular optional doesn't mean it's the right choice for you. Make an independent decision based on your strengths and interests.

Remember, the ideal optional subject varies from person to person. It's a subjective choice, and there's no one-size-fits-all answer. Take your time, evaluate your options based on the strategies mentioned above, and choose wisely.

TAILORED PATHS TO CSE: BEST APPROACHES FOR ARTS, ENGINEERING, MANAGEMENT, MEDICAL, AND SCIENCE STUDENTS

Choosing an optional subject for the UPSC Civil Services Examination (CSE) often hinges on an individual's personal interest, but it's also influenced by their academic background. Let's take a look at the optional subjects that might be more accessible or relatable to students from various academic disciplines:

1. **Arts Students:**

   - **History:** A natural choice for those who studied history during their undergraduate studies.

   - **Sociology:** A popular and scoring optional for those with a background in sociology or anthropology.

   - **Political Science and International Relations:** Suitable for those with a keen interest in politics, governance, and international affairs.

   - **Geography:** Has some overlap with GS papers, making it a beneficial choice.

   - **Philosophy or Psychology:** For those who have a penchant for understanding human nature, thought, and behavior.

2. **Engineering Students:**

   - **Mathematics:** Especially for those with strong analytical and problem-solving skills.

   - **Mechanical Engineering, Civil Engineering, Electrical Engineering:** UPSC offers these as optional subjects. Those with a corresponding engineering background can consider these.

   - **Anthropology:** A favorite among engineers due to its scientific approach and limited syllabus.

- **Geography:** The physical geography component can appeal to the analytical mind of an engineer.

3. Management Students:

- **Public Administration:** Offers insights into the administrative machinery, governance, and policy-making.

- **Sociology:** Provides a comprehensive understanding of society, institutions, and social behavior.

- **Anthropology:** An understanding of human evolution, society structures, and behavior.

- **Economics:** Especially if one has specialized in Business Economics or related fields during their MBA or BBA.

4. Medical Students:

- **Medical Science:** Directly aligned with their academic background.

- **Anthropology:** The biological anthropology part has sections related to human anatomy and evolution, which might be of interest to medical students.

- **Psychology:** Especially for those interested in psychiatry.

5. Science Students:

- **Physics, Chemistry, Botany, Zoology:** Direct options for those with bachelor's degrees in these subjects.

- **Geography:** Especially for those from Earth Sciences or Environmental Sciences backgrounds.

- **Mathematics or Statistics:** For those with a B.Sc. in these subjects or those who have a strong quantitative aptitude.

In the end, while one's academic background can offer an advantage in terms of familiarity, the most crucial factors remain personal interest, availability of resources, and the comfort level with the subject's content. Always review the syllabus and a few basic books before finalizing an optional, regardless of your academic background.

STAYING AHEAD OF THE CURVE: A GUIDE FOR CSE ASPIRANTS TO KEEP ABREAST WITH UPSC NOTIFICATIONS AND RELEVANT RESOURCES

Staying updated with UPSC's notifications is crucial for any CSE aspirant, as missing out on any crucial update can have detrimental effects on the preparation. Here are some strategies and resources to ensure you're always updated:

1. **UPSC's Official Website:**
   - **upsc.gov.in** This is the most authoritative source for all UPSC notifications, including exam schedules, syllabus changes, and result announcements. Aspirants should make it a habit to check the website regularly.

2. **Mobile Applications:**
   - **UPSC Official App:** This app, available on popular app stores, provides notifications, rcsults, exam schedules, and other details on the go.
   - **Other UPSC Preparation Apps:** Many private apps cater to UPSC aspirants and usually include a feature to provide UPSC notifications. Examples include ClearIAS, Unacademy, and mrunal.org's app.

3. **Online Forums and Websites:**
   - iasbaba.com
   - insightsonindia.com
   - forumias.com These websites regularly post updates about UPSC notifications and also have active forums where aspirants discuss recent developments.

4. **Telegram and WhatsApp Groups:** There are many groups dedicated to UPSC preparations. They can be a good source for real-time updates, but it's essential to verify the information from a second source.

5. **YouTube Channels:** Many educational channels on YouTube cater to UPSC aspirants. Some popular ones are Unacademy, Drishti IAS, and StudyIQ. They often release videos regarding the latest UPSC notifications.

6. **Newspapers:** National dailies, especially "The Hindu" and "The Indian Express", sometimes carry UPSC notifications, especially the significant ones like the release of exam dates or results.

7. **Email Alerts:** UPSC offers an option to subscribe to email alerts for various notifications. Make sure to use an email that you check regularly.

8. **Set Google Alerts:** You can set a Google alert for terms like "UPSC notification" or "UPSC CSE updates". This way, every time there's news or an article related to the terms, Google will send you an email alert.

9. **Social Media:** UPSC's official Twitter handle and other unofficial UPSC preparation groups on Facebook often share important notifications.

10. **Coaching Institutes:** If you're enrolled in a coaching institute, they usually have a system in place to inform students of any new UPSC notifications.

Given the importance of these notifications, it's a good strategy to have multiple channels of information. This way, even if you miss an update on one channel, the others will have you covered. Always remember to verify any information you receive from unofficial channels by checking the UPSC's official website.

DECODING THE UPSC CALENDAR: TIMING, NOTIFICATIONS, AND HOW THEY SHAPE A CSE ASPIRANT'S JOURNEY

The Union Public Service Commission (UPSC) generally follows a consistent annual calendar for its notifications and exams. Knowing these dates is beneficial for aspirants as it allows them to create an effective study schedule and be prepared for the examination process.

Here is a general outline of how UPSC usually releases its notifications and conducts exams, based on past patterns:

1. Annual Calendar Release:

UPSC releases its annual calendar almost a year in advance. For instance, the calendar for 2023 might be released in 2022. This calendar provides a tentative schedule for all exams conducted by UPSC throughout the year, including CSE (Civil Services Examination).

2. Civil Services (Preliminary) Examination:

- **Notification Release:** Usually in February.
- **Last Date for Receipt of Applications:** About 30 days from the release of the notification.
- **Date of Exam:** Typically in June.

3. Civil Services (Main) Examination:

- **Date of Exam:** Generally in September or October (only for those who qualify in the prelims).

4. Personality Test/Interview

For those who clear the Mains, usually scheduled between February to April of the following year.

5. **Final Results:** Typically announced a few weeks after the last interview.

Benefits of the UPSC Calendar for Aspirants:

1. **Study Schedule:** Aspirants can break down their syllabus and allocate specific months/weeks to each topic. It gives a clear timeline for both Prelims and Mains preparation.

2. **Mock Tests:** Knowing the exam dates in advance allows aspirants to schedule their mock tests accordingly, ensuring they are in peak performance mode close to the D-day.

3. **Application Preparation:** Aspirants can keep all necessary documents ready well in advance to avoid any last-minute issues during the application process.

4. **Balancing Optional & General Studies:** The schedule lets candidates allocate specific time for their optional subjects, which often requires focused preparation.

5. **Holistic Preparation:** With a clear understanding of the timeline, aspirants can allocate time for newspaper reading, current affairs, answer writing practice, and revision.

6. **Mental Preparation:** Knowing the dates can reduce anxiety and uncertainty. It gives aspirants a clear goal to work towards.

7. **Flexibility:** In case of any unforeseen personal events or emergencies, aspirants can adjust their preparation strategy based on the remaining time.

8. **Financial Planning:** For those taking coaching or planning to buy resources, knowing the exam dates can help in budgeting and financial planning.

However, it's important to note that while the UPSC is largely consistent, there can be changes or postponements, especially due to unforeseen events like national emergencies, natural disasters, or situations like the COVID-19 pandemic. Therefore, always keep an eye on the official UPSC website for the latest updates and changes.

MINING THE ARCHIVES: LOCATING AND ACCESSING UPSC'S PREVIOUS QUESTION PAPERS FOR CSE PREPARATION

Previous question papers for the UPSC Civil Services Examination (CSE) can be a vital resource for aspirants, as they provide insights into the pattern of questions, the level of difficulty, and the areas of focus in the syllabus. Here's where and how you can access them:

1. **UPSC Official Website:**

   ◆ The official website of the Union Public Service Commission (www.upsc.gov.in) provides question papers of the previous years for various examinations, including the Civil Services Preliminary and Main Examination.

   ◆ Navigate to the "Examination" tab on the main page and select "Previous Question Papers" from the dropdown menu.

   ◆ Choose the year and the specific exam you are interested in to download the question papers in PDF format.

2. **Books/Printed Material:**

   ◆ Several leading publications compile and sell UPSC previous years' question papers in book format, often with solutions. These are available in major bookstores and online e-commerce platforms.

   ◆ Popular titles include "UPSC Previous Years' Solved Papers" by various publishers.

3. **Online Education Platforms:**

   ◆ Numerous online education platforms and UPSC coaching websites provide previous years' question papers for free download or online practice. Some of these platforms include InsightsIAS, IASbaba, Unacademy, etc.

4. Mobile Apps:

- There are many mobile applications dedicated to UPSC preparation available on Android and iOS platforms. These apps often have a repository of past years' papers. Examples include "UPSC IAS All in One" and "ClearIAS" among others.

5. Libraries:

- Major libraries, especially those in cities known for UPSC preparation hubs (like Delhi), have a collection of past years' UPSC question papers in book format.

6. Coaching Institutes:

- If you're enrolled in a coaching institute, they usually provide their students with previous year papers as part of their study material.

Tips for Using Previous Year Papers:

1. **Analysis:** Before diving into solution books or discussions, try to solve the papers yourself. This will give you a realistic understanding of where you stand.

2. **Understand the Pattern:** Over the years, the pattern of questions might evolve. Observing these changes can give hints about UPSC's current focus areas.

3. **Timed Practice:** Solve the papers in a simulated exam environment, sticking to the actual duration of the exam. This will improve your time management skills.

4. **Revision:** Revisit the questions you found difficult or got wrong. This can guide your revision strategy.

5. **Consistent Practice:** Instead of cramming multiple papers close to the exam, it's better to solve them consistently throughout your preparation.

Always ensure you're referring to authentic sources when accessing previous year papers. The UPSC website is the most reliable source, but other reputable platforms can also be beneficial.

COLLECTIVE WISDOM: EVALUATING THE MERITS AND DRAWBACKS OF GROUP AND COMPREHENSIVE STUDY STRATEGIES FOR CSE ASPIRANTS

Group study, especially for a comprehensive examination like the UPSC Civil Services Examination (CSE), can be a double-edged sword. It has its merits and demerits. Whether an aspirant should engage in group study largely depends on his/her personal learning style and the dynamics of the group. Here's a critical review of group study for the UPSC CSE:

Advantages:

1. **Diverse Perspectives:** In a group, every individual might have a unique way of understanding or interpreting a topic. This diversity can provide a broader perspective, which is particularly helpful in GS papers and Essay writing.

2. **Resource Sharing:** Not every aspirant can buy or access every resource/ book. In group study, members can share their resources, notes, and references.

3. **Motivation:** Preparing for UPSC can be mentally taxing. Having peers who are on the same journey can serve as a morale boost. They can motivate each other during low phases.

4. **Clarifying Doubts:** If an aspirant has a doubt about a particular topic, it might get clarified in group discussions without the need for external help.

5. **Mock Interviews and Tests:** Group members can conduct mock interviews for each other, which can be a crucial preparatory step for the actual UPSC interview.

6. **Current Affairs Discussions:** Given the dynamic nature of current affairs, discussing recent events and their implications in a group can enhance understanding.

Disadvantages:

1. **Distractions:** If not properly managed, group studies can become more of a gossip session rather than a productive study time.

2. **Pace Mismatch:** Every aspirant has a different study speed. In a group setting, there might be pressure to match the group's pace, which can be detrimental.

3. **Over-dependence:** Some aspirants might become too dependent on the group for information and understanding, compromising their independent study time.

4. **Potential Conflicts:** Differences in opinion or approach can lead to conflicts which might waste precious time and also affect morale.

5. **Logistical Challenges:** Coordinating schedules and finding a suitable place for everyone to meet can be a challenge.

6. **Possible Misinformation:** If no one in the group is sure about a particular topic, there's a risk of circulating incorrect information among the members.

Points of Consideration:

1. **Choose Wisely:** If you're considering group study, choose members wisely. Ensure they are as committed as you are and that the group size remains manageable (usually 3-5 members).

2. **Define Goals:** Every study session should have clearly defined goals. It ensures the group remains on track.

3. **Regular Reviews:** Regularly review the effectiveness of group study. If it's more distracting than beneficial, it might be time to reconsider.

4. **Respect Individual Differences:** Remember that every aspirant is different. Respect these differences and use them to the group's advantage rather than letting them become points of contention.

5. **Blend with Individual Study:** Group study should complement, not replace, individual study. Dedicate ample time for self-study.

Conclusion: Group study, when approached correctly, can be a valuable tool in an aspirant's UPSC preparation arsenal. However, it's essential to regularly evaluate its effectiveness and make necessary adjustments. Every aspirant should weigh the pros and cons in light of their personal learning style and decide accordingly.

REFINING THE REVIEW PROCESS: SCIENTIFIC STRATEGIES FOR EFFICIENT REVISION OF NOTES AND MATERIALS FOR CSE ASPIRANTS

Effective revision is a critical component of any successful study strategy, especially for a comprehensive examination like the UPSC CSE. Incorporating scientific methods into the revision process can significantly enhance retention and understanding. Here are some scientifically-backed strategies that aspirants can use:

1. **Spaced Repetition:**
   - This involves reviewing information at increasing intervals over time. Instead of cramming, study a topic and then review it after a day, then a week, then a month, etc.
   - Tools like Anki or Quizlet use this technique, allowing you to create flashcards and then prompting you to review them at optimal intervals.

2. **Active Recall:**
   - This is the active process of retrieving information from memory without looking at the source.
   - Instead of just reading notes, close the book/notebook and try to recollect the main points. This effortful retrieval enhances long-term retention.

3. **Teaching or Feynman Technique:**
   - Try explaining the topic as if you were teaching it to someone else. If you struggle, it indicates areas you need to revisit.
   - Named after physicist Richard Feynman, the Feynman Technique is about simplifying concepts and explaining them in layman's terms.

4. Interleaved Learning:

- Instead of dedicating long hours to a single subject (blocked practice), mix up subjects or topics (interleaved practice).

- This has been found to be especially effective for subjects that involve problem-solving, like Mathematics.

5. Mind Mapping:

- This visual strategy involves creating diagrams to represent terms, ideas, tasks, or other items linked to and arranged around a central keyword or idea.

- Mind maps can help in connecting different pieces of information, thereby aiding holistic understanding.

6. Chunking Information:

- Breaking down information into bite-sized chunks can help in processing and understanding information better.

- For instance, instead of trying to remember a long list of points, group them into related categories.

7. Test Yourself:

- Regular self-testing can significantly boost retention. Use past year's papers, mock tests, or even flashcards.

- This engages active recall, strengthens neural connections, and highlights areas of weakness.

8. Elaborative Interrogation:

- This involves asking "how" and "why" questions as you study. For example, instead of just memorizing a fact, ask yourself why it's true or how it relates to what you already know.

9. Healthy Sleep Habits:

- Sleep is crucial for memory consolidation. Ensure you're getting adequate and quality sleep, especially after intensive study sessions.

10. Physical Activity:

- Regular physical activity has been shown to have various cognitive benefits, including improved memory and thinking skills.

11. Mindfulness and Meditation:

- ◆ Techniques like meditation can enhance concentration, attention span, and even cognitive flexibility, all of which are beneficial for revision.

12. Use of Mnemonics:

- ◆ Mnemonics are memory aids, often involving rhymes, songs, or associations. They can be especially handy for memorizing lists or sequences.

13. Healthy Diet:

- ◆ A balanced diet, including Omega-3 fatty acids, antioxidants, and other nutrients, can support cognitive functions and memory.

Conclusion: Scientifically-backed revision strategies can be transformative for CSE aspirants. However, it's essential to note that different techniques might work differently for each individual. Aspirants should experiment, adapt, and identify what combination of methods works best for them.

THE INTERPLAY OF CASTE AND RESERVATIONS: ANALYZING THEIR INFLUENCE ON CSE SUCCESS RATES AND THE UNDERLYING REASONS

The Civil Services Examination (CSE) conducted by the UPSC in India has a system of reservations for various social groups, primarily Scheduled Castes (SC), Scheduled Tribes (ST), Other Backward Classes (OBC), and Economically Weaker Sections (EWS). The reservation system has been a subject of both support and criticism over the years. Here's a critical analysis of how caste and reservation might influence the success rate in the CSE:

1. Historical Background:

The reservation system was introduced as a means of affirmative action to redress historical injustices and socio-economic disparities faced by marginalized communities. The intent was to ensure adequate representation in administrative services and other areas.

2. Impact on Success Rate:

- **Representation**: Reservation has undeniably enabled increased representation of historically marginalized groups in the civil services. This means that members from these categories have a higher chance of getting into services due to reserved seats.

- **Cut-off Marks**: The cut-off marks in preliminary and mains exams for reserved categories are generally lower than those for the unreserved/ general category. This gives reserved category candidates a relatively better chance of progressing through the stages of the exam.

- **Number of Attempts**: Reserved category candidates are allowed a higher number of attempts compared to general category candidates (with certain age relaxations too). This could potentially give them more opportunities to clear the exam.

3. Concerns and Criticisms:

◆ **Merit Argument**: Critics argue that reservation affects the principle of meritocracy. They contend that positions in the bureaucracy should be filled based purely on merit, irrespective of caste or socio-economic background.

◆ **Creamy Layer**: Within the OBC category, there's a debate about the 'creamy layer' (the relatively wealthier and more educated individuals). Critics believe that these individuals unduly benefit from the reservation system at the expense of the truly needy.

◆ **Perpetuation of Caste Identities**: Some argue that reservations might unintentionally perpetuate caste identities and divisions.

4. Counterarguments:

◆ **Holistic Merit**: Proponents of reservation argue that merit isn't just about exam scores. Experiences, diverse backgrounds, and the ability to empathize and understand the nuances of India's diverse populace are also part of an officer's merit.

◆ **Social Justice**: Reservation is seen as a tool for social justice. The argument is that a more representative bureaucracy will be more attuned to the needs of a diverse population.

◆ **Socio-Economic Factors**: Candidates from marginalized communities might not have access to the same resources, coaching, or even basic facilities as others. Reservation helps level the playing field.

Conclusion:

While caste and reservation can influence the success rate in the CSE due to the systemic provisions in place, it's essential to understand that these provisions were introduced as a means to achieve a more inclusive and representative bureaucracy. Over time, the dynamics of reservation, its implications, and its future course will remain subjects of debate and evaluation in India. As of now, reservation is one of the many factors that influence the CSE's outcome, but success in these exams requires dedication, preparation, and hard work, irrespective of category.

CSE SELECTION DYNAMICS: THE ROLES OF CASTE, ATTEMPT LIMITS, AGE RELAXATIONS, AND OTHER FACTORS

Certainly! Here's a table illustrating the relaxation criteria for different categories in the UPSC Civil Services Examination as of my last update in 2021:

Category	Number of Attempts	Age Relaxation	Other Benefits
General (Unreserved)	6	Up to 32 years	None
OBC	9	Up to 35 years	Cumulative Age Relaxation (i.e., if an OBC candidate is also a person with Benchmark Disability, then the age relaxation is a cumulative addition of OBC + PwBD)
SC/ST	Unlimited till age limit	Up to 37 years	Cumulative Age Relaxation (for PwBD SC/ST candidates)
Economically Weaker Sections (EWS)	6	Up to 32 years	None
Persons with Benchmark Disability (General)	9	Up to 42 years	Can avail services of a scribe

Persons with Benchmark Disability (OBC)	9	Up to 45 years	Can avail services of a scribe
Persons with Benchmark Disability (SC/ST)	Unlimited till age limit	Up to 47 years	Can avail services of a scribe
Ex-Servicemen (General)	6	Up to 32 years + Service rendered	Counted as an attempt if appeared even once
Ex-Servicemen (OBC)	9	Up to 35 years + Service rendered	Counted as an attempt if appeared even once
Ex-Servicemen (SC/ST)	Unlimited till age limit	Up to 37 years + Service rendered	Counted as an attempt if appeared even once
Jammu & Kashmir Domiciled (General)	6	Up to 37 years	None
Jammu & Kashmir Domiciled (OBC)	9	Up to 40 years	None
Jammu & Kashmir Domiciled (SC/ST)	Unlimited till age limit	Up to 42 years	None

Note: These numbers are based on the UPSC notification as of 2021. The criteria can change depending on the commission's decisions and any modifications to government policies. Aspirants should always refer to the official UPSC notification for the most recent and accurate details.

DISSECTING CSE SELECTION: DEMYSTIFYING CLAIMS OF BIAS, CORRUPTION, AND POLLUTION IN THE RECRUITMENT PROCESS

The UPSC Civil Services Examination (CSE) is one of the most prestigious and challenging competitive exams in India. Due to its importance in recruiting for key positions in the Indian bureaucracy, its process and outcomes are sometimes scrutinized, debated, and even criticized. Let's break down some of the concerns and provide an understanding of the CSE selection process:

1. Selection Process:

The CSE selection process comprises three stages: a. **Preliminary Examination:** An objective-type test that serves as a screening tool. b. **Mains Examination:** An essay and subjective-type paper examination. c. **Personal Interview:** Assesses the personal attributes of candidates.

2. Criticism and Concerns:

a. **Opaque Evaluation in Mains**: Since the Mains exam involves subjective answers, candidates often express concerns about the transparency of the evaluation process. There have been demands to make the evaluated answer sheets public.

b. **Bias in Interviews:** Some candidates feel that there might be biases in the interview stage based on the candidate's background, appearance, accent, or region.

c. **Syllabus and Question Pattern:** Changes in the syllabus or the pattern of questions sometimes generate criticism, especially if candidates feel unprepared for these changes.

d. **Reservation System:** India's reservation policy, meant to uplift historically marginalized communities, often becomes a point of debate. Critics argue it may not be the most efficient method of ensuring social justice, while proponents see it as essential.

e. **Age and Attempt Limit:** The cap on the number of attempts and age limits, especially for the general category, has been a point of contention.

f. **Language and Medium:** The removal of certain regional languages as a medium for the exam has been contentious. Similarly, there has been criticism about the translation of questions, especially in the compulsory English and Hindi language papers.

3. Validity of Criticisms:

a. **Transparency:** UPSC is an autonomous constitutional body, and it has mechanisms to ensure the utmost transparency and fairness. For instance, to avoid bias, the interview board does not have access to candidates' marks in Mains, ensuring an unbiased assessment.

b. **Standardization Process:** To tackle potential biases in the interview, UPSC uses a process of standardization and moderation, where marks are adjusted to ensure uniformity in evaluation across panels.

c. **Reservation:** The reservation policy is a constitutional provision, and UPSC adheres to it to ensure representation and inclusivity.

d. **Continuous Revision:** UPSC frequently revises the syllabus, question patterns, and other processes to remain up-to-date and maintain the examination's standard.

Conclusion

While concerns and criticisms are natural given the high stakes of the CSE, it's crucial to understand that UPSC operates with a high degree of integrity and professionalism. It consistently works towards refining and improving the selection process. However, like any system, it's not impervious to challenges and issues, and constructive feedback is essential for its evolution.

UPSC'S PROACTIVE RESPONSE: MEASURES AND EVALUATIONS TO COUNTER CRITICISMS AND ENSURE A TRANSPARENT SELECTION PROCESS

The UPSC has always been aware of the criticisms directed at it and has taken various steps over the years to address these concerns, ensuring that the CSE remains a transparent, fair, and robust system. Here's a critical evaluation of some of the measures UPSC has undertaken:

1. **Digital Evaluation:** To ensure transparency and reduce human error, UPSC introduced a digital evaluation system for the Mains examination. This involves scanning the answer sheets and then evaluating them on computers, thus ensuring quicker and more transparent evaluation.

2. **Blind Assessment:** To ensure that there's no bias during the evaluation of Mains answer sheets, the identity of the candidates remains anonymous. Evaluators do not have access to any personal information about the candidates whose papers they are assessing.

3. **Diverse Interview Boards:** The UPSC ensures that the interview boards are diverse, comprising members from various backgrounds, ensuring that no inherent bias creeps into the interview process.

4. **Continuous Training of Evaluators:** UPSC regularly conducts workshops and training sessions for paper evaluators to ensure that they follow uniform criteria and standards. This reduces subjectivity in the Mains paper evaluation.

5. **Feedback Mechanism:** UPSC has set up mechanisms to receive feedback from candidates about various stages of the examination process. This helps the commission in making necessary changes and improvements.

6. **Periodic Review of Syllabus and Pattern:** UPSC periodically reviews the syllabus and exam pattern. For instance, the introduction of the CSAT

(Civil Services Aptitude Test) in Prelims was one such change to test analytical skills and aptitude in addition to knowledge.

7. **Language Policy:** Despite criticisms, UPSC has tried to ensure that candidates from all linguistic backgrounds have a fair shot. Though there have been changes in the language policy, candidates can still answer the Mains examination (except the compulsory language papers) in a language of their choice from the Eighth Schedule of the Indian Constitution.

8. **Representation from Various Quarters:** UPSC panels often include members from diverse socio-economic, regional, and professional backgrounds. This ensures a holistic understanding and evaluation of policies and practices.

9. **Liaising with Training Institutes:** The UPSC coordinates with various training institutes like the Lal Bahadur Shastri National Academy of Administration (LBSNAA) to ensure that the training modules are updated and in line with the current needs of the administration.

Conclusion:

The UPSC is not a static body and evolves based on the feedback and needs of the time. While it has made many progressive changes, it's essential to remember that it operates within a larger framework of policies, rules, and constitutional mandates. The balance it strikes between maintaining tradition and incorporating change is a testament to its commitment to selecting the best candidates for the Indian civil services in the fairest manner possible.

North vs. South: Assessing the Alleged Disparities in CSE Success Rates and Delving into the Underlying Factors:

The criticism or perception that candidates from North India have a higher success rate in the UPSC Civil Services Examination (CSE) compared to those from South India has been a topic of discussion in various circles. Here's a nuanced understanding of this perception:

1. Historical Context:

- In the initial years post-independence, North India, especially states like Uttar Pradesh, Bihar, and Rajasthan, had a significant representation in the UPSC selected candidates. This was because of the historical prominence of cities like Allahabad and Delhi as hubs for civil services preparation.

- The coaching culture in these cities, especially Delhi, solidified this trend. Over time, a support system evolved, with libraries, coaching centers, and study circles catering exclusively to civil services aspirants.

2. Language and Medium of Examination:

- Earlier, English and Hindi were the dominant mediums of examination. Candidates from Hindi-speaking states naturally had an advantage when taking the exam in Hindi.

- However, UPSC has made efforts to level the playing field. Now candidates can take the examination in any of the languages listed in the Eighth Schedule of the Indian Constitution. This has provided an impetus for candidates from various linguistic backgrounds, including South India, to compete.

3. Perception vs. Reality:

- The actual data of successful candidates over the past decade indicates a more diverse representation from various states. States like Kerala, Tamil Nadu, Andhra Pradesh, and Karnataka have seen multiple toppers and consistent selections in the UPSC CSE.

- The claim might be rooted more in perception than in sustained reality.

4. Shift in Trend:

- Over the years, there's been a discernible shift. Cities like Hyderabad, Bengaluru, and Thiruvananthapuram are emerging as new hubs for UPSC preparation, with quality coaching centers and study resources available.

5. Socio-Economic Factors:

- States in North India, especially Bihar and Uttar Pradesh, traditionally viewed the civil services as a prestigious and viable career option. The socio-economic conditions drove many to see government jobs, especially the IAS and IPS, as means of social mobility.

- On the other hand, South Indian states, with their diverse economic base, had multiple career avenues, from IT to healthcare, for their youth.

6. Role of State Governments:

- Some state governments, especially in the south, have initiated programs and training centers to help aspirants from their states succeed in UPSC exams. This has further balanced the representation.

Conclusion

While historical trends may have shown a particular skew, the scenario has become more balanced in recent years. Success in the UPSC CSE is less about regional representation and more about individual perseverance, preparation, and aptitude. It's crucial to approach the topic with data-driven insights rather than regional biases.

NAVIGATING CSE UNCERTAINTIES: COMMON APPREHENSIONS AND CONCERNS FOR ASPIRANTS

Civil Services Examination (CSE) aspirants often face a multitude of apprehensions and concerns as they navigate the highly competitive and demanding nature of the examination process. Here are some common apprehensions:

1. **Vast Syllabus:**

   - The CSE covers a broad range of topics from history, geography, polity, economy, to current affairs, making the syllabus vast and sometimes intimidating for aspirants.

2. **High Competition:**

   - Every year, lakhs of candidates appear for the preliminary examination, competing for a limited number of positions, making the CSE one of the toughest exams globally.

3. **Number of Attempts:**

   - With restrictions on the number of attempts (usually six for general category candidates and with certain age limits), many aspirants worry about exhausting their attempts without success.

4. **Choice of Optional Subject:**

   - The choice of the optional subject is a major decision as it can significantly influence the final score. Aspirants often grapple with the dilemma of choosing a subject they're passionate about versus one that is perceived as 'scoring'.

5. Language Barrier:

- ◆ Candidates from non-English medium backgrounds sometimes fear they might be at a disadvantage. Though UPSC allows candidates to write the exam in various languages, the availability and quality of study material might be a concern.

6. Financial Constraints:

- ◆ Preparing for CSE can be financially draining, especially for those who opt for coaching. The cost of study materials, mock tests, and living expenses (for those relocating for coaching) can be substantial.

7. Duration of Preparation:

- ◆ The CSE process, from preliminary to interview, is long. Many aspirants are apprehensive about investing years in preparation with no guaranteed outcome.

8. Balancing Job/Studies with Preparation:

- ◆ Those who prepare while working or pursuing other courses often find it challenging to manage time effectively.

9. Changing Exam Patterns:

- ◆ UPSC occasionally modifies the pattern, syllabus, or nature of questions, making it unpredictable and adding to the aspirants' anxiety.

10. Social Pressure and Expectations:

- ◆ The societal prestige associated with civil services in India means aspirants often face immense pressure from family and peers. The fear of not meeting these expectations can be mentally taxing.

11. Physical and Mental Well-being:

- ◆ The rigorous preparation often means long hours of study, leading to concerns about health, stress, and burnout.

12. Doubts About Personal Abilities:

- ◆ Given the demanding nature of the exam, moments of self-doubt are common where aspirants question their capabilities and preparation strategies.

13. Lack of Structured Guidance:

- **Apprehension**: Especially for those who cannot afford coaching, the absence of structured guidance can be daunting.

- **Overcome Strategy**: Leveraging online platforms, like free YouTube lectures, UPSC dedicated forums, or free course materials available online, can provide structured preparation. Engaging in peer groups or study circles can also provide collaborative learning and support.

14. Failure and its Aftermath:

- **Apprehension**: The thought of not clearing the exam after months or years of preparation can be a significant concern.

- **Overcome Strategy**: Developing a growth mindset is crucial. Viewing each attempt as a learning experience rather than a failure can change the approach. Having a backup plan or parallel career goal can also reduce anxiety.

15. Isolation During Preparation:

- **Apprehension**: Intensive preparation often means cutting back on social interactions, which can lead to feelings of loneliness.

- **Overcome Strategy**: Scheduling regular short breaks, engaging in group studies, and setting aside time for leisure and family can ensure aspirants don't feel too isolated.

16. Staying Updated with Current Affairs:

- **Apprehension**: The dynamic nature of current affairs can be overwhelming for some.

- **Overcome Strategy**: Regularly following one or two trusted news sources, using apps that curate UPSC-relevant news, and creating notes can help. Monthly magazines dedicated to UPSC preparation can also be beneficial.

17. Handling Negative Peer Pressure:

- **Apprehension**: Seeing peers succeeding in other professions or hearing about their achievements can create doubts.

- **Overcome Strategy**: Remembering that every individual's journey is unique and focusing on one's personal goals and growth can be crucial. Avoiding unnecessary comparisons is key.

18. Fear of the Interview:

- **Apprehension**: Even after clearing the written exams, the interview or the personality test can be a significant cause of stress.

- **Overcome Strategy**: Engaging in mock interviews, staying updated with current events, and developing good communication skills can be beneficial. Being genuine and maintaining a calm demeanor during the interview is crucial.

19. Time Management Issues:

- **Apprehension**: Balancing between different subjects and ensuring adequate revision time can be challenging.

- **Overcome Strategy**: Creating a realistic timetable, prioritizing subjects based on strengths and weaknesses, and setting weekly targets can help manage time efficiently.

20. Lack of Motivation Over Time:

- **Apprehension**: The long duration of preparation can lead to dips in motivation.

- **Overcome Strategy**: Regularly revisiting the reason for choosing civil services, watching motivational talks, or reading about successful IAS officers can rekindle motivation.

21. Dependency on Coaching Institutes:

- **Apprehension**: Over-relying on coaching institutes can sometimes hinder self-study and personal understanding.

- **Overcome Strategy**: While coaching can provide direction, it's essential to complement it with self-study. Practice and revision are key and should be done personally.

By understanding these apprehensions and proactively addressing them, aspirants can have a more balanced and focused preparation phase. To mitigate these apprehensions, aspirants are advised to seek guidance from mentors, former candidates, or coaching institutions. Peer support, structured planning, regular breaks, and physical activity can also help in maintaining a balanced preparation phase.

BEYOND THE RUMORS: DISSECTING ASSUMPTIONS, MYTHS, AND REALITIES SURROUNDING THE CSE FROM AN ASPIRANT'S PERSPECTIVE

The UPSC Civil Services Examination (CSE) is one of the most prestigious and challenging examinations in India, and understandably, there are many myths, assumptions, and realities associated with it. Let's explore these from the perspective of aspirants:

Assumptions:

1. **Long Study Hours Guarantee Success**: Many assume that studying 14-16 hours a day guarantees success.

2. **Coaching is Mandatory**: Many believe that without coaching, cracking the CSE is impossible.

3. **English Medium Students Have an Edge**: There's an assumption that students from an English medium background perform better in CSE.

4. **Only First Attempts are Successful**: Some think if they don't clear in the first attempt, chances of success in later attempts are slim.

Myths:

1. **CSE Requires Memorization**: The myth is that rote memorization of facts, dates, and events will lead to success.

2. **One Needs to Know Everything**: Some believe they need to master every topic under the sun to crack the CSE.

3. **CSE is Only for Top Students**: There's a prevalent myth that only academically brilliant students can succeed in the CSE.

4. **Optional Subject Decides Success**: Some aspirants believe that success in CSE heavily relies on the choice of the optional subject.

5. **Success in Prelims Guarantees Success in Mains/Interview**: Some think that doing well in the preliminary exam ensures overall success.

Realities:

1. **Consistency is Key**: More than long study hours, what matters is consistent and qualitative study.

2. **Understanding is Important**: UPSC tests understanding and analytical skills, not rote memorization.

3. **Many Successful Candidates are Self-prepared**: While coaching can provide guidance, many candidates have cracked CSE with self-study.

4. **Diverse Backgrounds**: Successful candidates come from diverse educational, linguistic, and regional backgrounds.

5. **Importance of Mock Tests**: Regular mock tests and answer writing practice play a crucial role in preparation.

6. **UPSC is Unpredictable**: The nature of questions asked in UPSC can be unpredictable, and success might require multiple attempts.

7. **Holistic Development**: UPSC isn't just about academic knowledge. It tests a candidate's overall personality, including their opinions, values, and interpersonal skills.

8. **Health and Mental Well-being**: Due to the rigorous nature of the exam, maintaining physical and mental health is essential.

Assumptions:

1. **Background Matters**: There's an assumption that those from premier institutes or metropolitan cities have a better shot.

2. **Current Affairs Means Newspaper Only**: Many believe that just reading a newspaper is enough for current affairs.

3. **UPSC Prefers Certain Optional Subjects**: Some think UPSC has a bias towards certain optional subjects, making them scoring.

4. **Interview is a Test of Knowledge**: Some assume that the personality test/ interview is another test of knowledge, similar to prelims or mains.

Myths:

1. **Reading More Books Equals Better Preparation**: The myth that the more books one refers to, the better their preparation.

2. **One Needs to Be Fluent in English**: A misconception that fluency in English is necessary to succeed.

3. **Age Equals Maturity in Interview**: Some believe older candidates are considered more mature or serious in interviews.

4. **Civil Services is the Ultimate Career**: Some may view the civil services as the pinnacle of all careers, overshadowing other equally significant options.

5. **Always Follow Toppers' Strategies**: A myth that following the strategy of toppers to the letter will ensure success.

Realities:

1. **Customized Strategy**: What works for one aspirant might not work for another. Personalizing one's strategy is key.

2. **Depth over Breadth**: Instead of reading multiple sources, it's about understanding and analyzing a limited set of resources deeply.

3. **Continuous Adaptation**: Due to changing patterns and unpredictability, aspirants must be adaptable in their preparation.

4. **Value Addition is Crucial**: Simply reading is not enough. One needs to add value through insights, examples, and analysis.

5. **Emphasis on Ethics and Integrity**: Especially in the mains and interview stages, UPSC places a lot of emphasis on a candidate's ethical standpoint and integrity.

6. **Failure Can Be a Stepping Stone**: Many who eventually top the exam might not have succeeded in their first or even second attempt. Every attempt, regardless of the outcome, adds to the experience.

7. **Mental Resilience**: Due to the nature and length of the examination process, mental stamina and resilience are as crucial as academic preparation.

Aspirants should ideally separate the wheat from the chaff, focusing on what's crucial and avoiding common misconceptions. This will not only streamline their preparation but also improve their chances of success. Understanding the realities and dispelling myths is crucial for aspirants to approach the exam with the right mindset and strategy.

DEBUNKING MYTHS AND CRAFTING SUCCESS: STRATEGIES FOR NAVIGATING MISCONCEPTIONS AND EXCELLING IN THE CSE

Certainly. Let's address each assumption and myth, providing strategies to overcome them:

Assumptions:

1. Background Matters:

- **Overcoming Strategy**: Understand that UPSC assesses a candidate's present capability, not their past educational background. Plenty of candidates from rural backgrounds and non-premier institutes have topped the exam.

2. Current Affairs Means Newspaper Only:

- **Overcoming Strategy**: Diversify your sources. Use online platforms, magazines, and AIR news summaries. Join current affairs discussion groups to get multiple perspectives.

3. UPSC Prefers Certain Optional Subjects:

- **Overcoming Strategy**: Choose an optional subject based on your interest and material availability, not popular opinion. Every subject has toppers; consistency and dedication matter.

4. Interview is a Test of Knowledge:

- **Overcoming Strategy**: Recognize that the interview assesses your personality, honesty, and suitability for the services. Be genuine and focus on being a balanced individual.

Myths:

1. Reading More Books Equals Better Preparation:

- ◆ **Overcoming Strategy**: Prioritize depth over breadth. Focus on understanding concepts deeply from limited, trusted resources rather than skimming through multiple books.

2. One Needs to Be Fluent in English:

- ◆ **Overcoming Strategy**: Remember that the exam can be taken in multiple languages. Your regional language or mother tongue can be just as effective if you're more comfortable with it.

3. Age Equals Maturity in Interview:

- ◆ **Overcoming Strategy**: Maturity is about experiences, perspectives, and how you present yourself. Age is just a number. Prepare well, and express your viewpoints clearly.

4. Civil Services is the Ultimate Career:

- ◆ **Overcoming Strategy**: Recognize that Civil Services is one among many noble and impactful professions. While it offers a unique platform, there are many ways to serve society and make a mark.

5. Always Follow Toppers' Strategies:

- ◆ **Overcoming Strategy**: Take inspiration but customize it according to your strengths, weaknesses, and situation. What works for one person might not work for another.

Overarching Strategies for Success:

1. **Self-awareness**: Understand your strengths and weaknesses. Tailor your preparation strategy accordingly.

2. **Regular Revision**: Information retention is critical. Set aside time for weekly, monthly, and quarterly revisions.

3. **Practice Answer Writing**: For mains, the way you structure and present your answer matters as much as your knowledge.

4. **Stay Updated, Stay Engaged**: Join discussion groups, attend seminars, and engage in intellectual discussions. This helps in broadening your perspective.

5. **Mock Tests**: Regularly attempt mock tests to get a real-time assessment of your preparation.

6. **Physical and Mental Well-being**: Regular exercise, meditation, and proper sleep can significantly enhance productivity and focus.

7. **Stay Positive**: Stay away from negativity. Surround yourself with positive, like-minded individuals.

8. **Consistency is Key**: It's not about studying 15 hours a day, but rather studying effectively and consistently.

Assumptions:

1. Duration of Study Matters:

- ◆ **Overcoming Strategy**: Quality over quantity. Consistent focused study for a few hours can be more productive than irregular and long hours of unfocused study.

2. Previous Year's Cut-off is a Good Benchmark:

- ◆ **Overcoming Strategy**: While previous year's cut-off gives an idea, the difficulty level of papers varies year to year. Instead, focus on giving your best without overly relying on past trends.

Myths:

1. Only People With Brilliant Academic Records Can Clear UPSC:

- ◆ **Overcoming Strategy**: UPSC tests understanding, analytical skills, and a broad perspective. Many who did not have a remarkable academic history have cleared and even topped the exam.

2. You Must Quit Your Job to Prepare:

- ◆ **Overcoming Strategy**: Many working professionals have cleared UPSC. Proper time management, focused study during weekends, and effective use of leave days can make a significant difference.

3. More Hours of Study Ensures Success:

- ◆ **Overcoming Strategy**: Efficiency is crucial. It's better to have 5 hours of highly productive study than 10 hours of distracted and unproductive study.

4. You Need to Know Everything:

- ◆ **Overcoming Strategy**: UPSC syllabus is vast, but it's about understanding rather than rote learning. Prioritize topics based on importance and your strengths.

Overarching Strategies:

1. **Personalize Your Strategy**: Everyone has their own pace and style of learning. Don't compare your progress with others.

2. **Stay Updated with Exam Pattern and Trends**: UPSC occasionally tweaks the pattern or emphasizes different areas. Being adaptable is beneficial.

3. **Continuous Feedback Loop**: Regularly evaluate your performance, understand areas of improvement, and adjust your strategy.

4. **Avoid Multiple Resources for a Single Topic**: This can lead to confusion. Pick one trusted resource and complement it with current affairs.

5. **Balanced Preparation**: While focusing on weak areas, ensure you also keep sharpening your strengths.

6. **Limit Social Media**: While some platforms might be beneficial for preparation, excessive use can be a distraction.

7. **Seek Guidance**: Engaging with mentors, joining discussion forums, or being part of study groups can give fresh perspectives and clear doubts.

8. **Breaks are Important**: Continuous study can lead to burnout. Regular short breaks, hobbies, or even walks can refresh the mind.

Remember, UPSC preparation is a marathon, not a sprint. Resilience, adaptability, and a genuine interest in understanding the diverse subjects are key. By keeping these strategies in mind and diligently applying them in your preparation, you enhance your chances of being among the successful candidates in the UPSC CSE.

Impacting Change as a CSE Officer: Harnessing Strengths, Addressing Weaknesses, and Strategies to Maximize Potential:

Civil Services Examination (CSE) qualifiers, particularly when they get selected into prestigious services like IAS, IPS, IFS, etc., are in a unique position to bring about impactful changes in society. Let's look at how, where, and the strengths and weaknesses associated:

How and Where a CSE Selected Person Can Make a Difference:

1. **Policy Formulation**: At the central and state levels, officers can help in formulating policies that have a long-term impact on the lives of millions.

2. **Implementation of Schemes**: Be it schemes related to health, education, or public welfare, officers ensure they are implemented properly.

3. **Disaster Management**: During natural disasters, officers coordinate relief and rehabilitation efforts.

4. **Maintaining Law and Order**: Particularly for IPS officers, ensuring peace and tranquillity is a primary responsibility.

5. **International Relations**: IFS officers represent India abroad, fostering diplomatic ties and furthering India's interests.

6. **Social Justice**: Ensuring that the benefits of government schemes reach the downtrodden, marginalized, and those in need.

7. **Innovation**: Introducing innovative solutions and technology for better governance and public service.

Strengths of a CSE Selected Officer:

1. **Authority**: Holding significant power to take decisions that can influence public life.

2. **Network**: Being part of a large network of officers across the country.

3. **Training**: Rigorous training provided at institutions like LBSNAA equips them with various skills.

4. **Public Trust**: Often, the public perceives them as beacons of hope.

5. **Resources**: Access to government resources to implement projects and schemes.

Weaknesses/Challenges:

1. **Bureaucratic Hurdles**: Red tape can sometimes slow down the decision-making process.

2. **Political Pressure**: Officers sometimes face pressures from political entities which might hinder unbiased, just administration.

3. **Lack of Specialized Knowledge**: While they receive broad-based training, they might lack expertise in specialized domains.

4. **Public Scrutiny**: Every action is under public and media scrutiny, which can be stressful.

5. **Transfers & Stability**: Frequent transfers can disrupt continuity in projects.

Overcoming Weaknesses:

1. **Continuous Learning**: Officers can enroll in courses or programs that give them specialized knowledge.

2. **Networking**: Building strong relationships with peers, seniors, and subordinates can help in navigating bureaucratic and political challenges.

3. **Engage with the Public**: Regular public interactions can garner support and feedback.

4. **Leverage Technology**: To bring in transparency, reduce red tape, and enhance efficiency.

5. **Seek Mentoring**: Senior officers can provide guidance on handling challenging situations.

An officer's journey is filled with opportunities and challenges. The impact they can make is profound, and the journey, while demanding, can be deeply satisfying.

Here are additional interventions and measures that can enhance the role of a CSE selected officer and help them navigate challenges:

Interventions to Enhance Impact:

1. **Stakeholder Collaboration**: Collaborating with NGOs, civil society organizations, and private entities can drive better results for public projects and initiatives.

2. **Feedback Mechanisms**: Instituting mechanisms to gather public feedback can ensure that projects are tailored to actual needs and can be adjusted based on real-world outcomes.

3. **Capacity Building**: Organizing regular training sessions and workshops for subordinate staff can improve the overall efficiency and impact of the administration.

4. **Public Awareness Campaigns**: Driving awareness about governmental policies, rights, and schemes ensures better uptake and a more informed citizenry.

5. **Digital Governance**: Implementing e-governance solutions can streamline public service delivery, making it more efficient and transparent.

6. **Ethical Standards**: Upholding and promoting high ethical standards in governance can foster trust and reduce corruption.

Interventions to Navigate Challenges:

1. **Conflict Resolution Training**: Equip officers with skills to mediate and resolve conflicts, whether they are community disputes or disagreements with political entities.

2. **Wellness Programs**: Given the stressful nature of the job, officers should have access to mental health and wellness resources.

3. **Transparent Communication**: Establishing open channels of communication with the public and media can reduce misconceptions and build trust.

4. **Mentoring Programs**: Connect junior officers with more experienced officers who can guide them, providing insights based on their experiences.

5. **Decentralization**: Empower lower levels of bureaucracy with decision-making powers for faster resolution and implementation.

6. **Inter-departmental Collaboration**: Ensuring different governmental departments work in tandem can reduce red tape and improve efficiency.

7. **Whistleblower Protections**: Ensure officers have the ability and protection to report any unethical activities or pressures they might encounter.

By incorporating these interventions and being adaptive to the evolving challenges, civil servants can remain effective, impactful, and continue to serve the best interests of the public.

THE HOLISTIC ASPIRANT: UNDERSTANDING THE PSYCHOLOGICAL, MENTAL, EMOTIONAL, PHYSICAL, AND MORAL CAPACITIES ESSENTIAL FOR CSE SUCCESS AND THEIR INFLUENCE ON ACHIEVEMENT RATES

Certainly, cracking the Civil Services Exam (CSE) is as much a test of one's knowledge as it is of one's character, emotional stability, and physical endurance. Here's a breakdown of the capabilities required and their influence on an aspirant's chances:

Psychological & Mental Capabilities:

1. **Adaptability**: CSE demands understanding and retaining a wide range of topics. An aspirant's ability to adapt to different subjects and retain diverse information is crucial.

2. **Resilience**: Not everyone clears the CSE in their first attempt. Mental toughness and resilience help aspirants persevere through multiple attempts.

3. **Analytical Thinking**: The nature of the questions requires not just rote learning but also analytical and critical thinking.

4. **Concentration**: With vast syllabi and hours of study needed, the ability to focus for extended periods is essential.

Emotional Capabilities:

1. **Emotional Stability**: Handling the pressure of the exam and the anticipation of results require emotional balance.

2. **Empathy**: This is especially crucial for the interview round, where interpersonal skills are tested.

3. **Stress Management**: The CSE journey can be long and taxing; managing one's stress is key to maintaining efficiency.

Physical Capabilities:

1. **Stamina**: Long hours of study and revision demand physical endurance.

2. **Health Management**: Regular physical activity and a balanced diet can aid cognition and concentration.

Moral Capabilities:

1. **Integrity**: A civil servant must be honest and principled. Demonstrating these qualities can also be beneficial during the interview phase.

2. **Ethical Reasoning**: This can set one apart in the mains and interview where nuanced questions on ethics are asked.

Other Capabilities:

1. **Time Management**: With vast syllabi, managing one's time becomes paramount.

2. **Interpersonal Skills**: Useful for group studies, interactions, and the interview phase.

Adopting these Capabilities:

1. **Routine Development**: A fixed study routine can help in improving concentration and adaptability.

2. **Mindfulness and Meditation**: To improve emotional stability, stress management, and concentration.

3. **Engage in Discussions**: Helps in building interpersonal skills and understanding diverse perspectives.

4. **Mock Exams & Reviews**: Helps in building stamina, resilience, and understanding one's strengths and weaknesses.

5. **Ethical Studies**: Engaging with case studies on ethics can hone moral reasoning skills.

Influence on Success Rate:

Each of these capabilities directly or indirectly impacts the success rate. For instance:

- Good mental health and resilience might mean that an aspirant doesn't get disheartened after a failed attempt and tries again.

- Analytical thinking can make the difference in scoring those few extra marks that separate a selected candidate from others.

- Physical health ensures an aspirant doesn't fall ill during crucial times and can put in consistent effort.

While knowledge is fundamental, these personal and character attributes play a significant role in determining the success of a CSE aspirant. It's a comprehensive test of an individual's character, aptitude, and knowledge.

URBAN VS. RURAL ASPIRANTS: DISSECTING THE PERCEIVED SUCCESS DISPARITY BETWEEN TIER I, II, III CITIES AND RURAL CONTENDERS IN THE CSE JOURNEY

The apprehension that aspirants from tier I, II, III cities have a higher success rate in the Civil Services Examination (CSE) compared to those from rural areas is a topic that has been debated for years. Let's critically evaluate this statement considering various aspects:

Reasons Supporting the Apprehension:

1. **Access to Coaching Institutes**: Tier I, II, and III cities often have well-established coaching centers which can guide aspirants in their preparation. This access can provide a structured approach to the vast syllabus.

2. **Resources**: Cities usually provide better access to libraries, books, newspapers, and internet facilities, which are crucial for preparation.

3. **Peer Group**: Being in an urban area often means being around more people preparing for the same examination, which can help in group studies, discussions, and moral support.

4. **Awareness**: The awareness about the examination, its benefits, and how to approach it might be higher in urban areas due to more exposure.

Counter-Arguments:

1. **Self-Study and Determination**: Many aspirants from rural areas have cleared the CSE relying predominantly on self-study. Their determination and focused approach often compensate for the lack of resources.

2. **Diverse Experience**: Candidates from rural backgrounds can bring in diverse experiences and perspectives, which can be an advantage in the interview round.

3. **Digital Penetration**: With the growing penetration of the internet and smartphones, many online resources, coaching classes, and guidance have become accessible to rural aspirants.

4. **Success Stories**: There are numerous instances where aspirants from remote villages and small towns have secured top ranks in CSE, proving that the place of origin is not the sole determinant of success.

Critical Evaluation:

◆   While it's true that urban areas, due to their infrastructural advantages, can offer aspirants certain benefits in terms of preparation, it doesn't automatically translate to success. The CSE is a test of one's knowledge, analytical skills, and personality, which aren't solely shaped by one's environment.

◆   It's also worth noting that challenges faced by rural aspirants can shape resilience and determination, traits valuable for any rigorous examination.

◆   The evolving digital landscape is rapidly bridging the urban-rural divide in terms of access to resources. Online platforms, webinars, e-books, and forums are democratizing CSE preparation.

◆   The core of the issue also touches upon the larger socio-economic disparities in India. While urban centers have better amenities, they also come with their set of challenges, such as distractions and competitive pressures.

In conclusion, while urban aspirants might have certain advantages in terms of accessibility and resources, success in the CSE is ultimately a combination of individual effort, strategy, and determination. The narrative of urban aspirants being more successful than rural ones is neither an absolute myth nor an undisputed reality. It's a nuanced issue with multiple facets, and while regional disparities exist, individual stories of determination from both spheres stand testament to the fact that success in CSE is not confined to any specific geography.

THE ANATOMY OF ELIGIBILITY: UNDERSTANDING CSE CRITERIA, THE IMPACT OF CRIMINAL HISTORY, AND OTHER KEY CONSIDERATIONS IN THE SELECTION PROCESS

The Civil Services Examination (CSE) conducted by the Union Public Service Commission (UPSC) in India has specific eligibility criteria for aspirants. Let's go over the eligibility criteria and some aspects which might impact an aspirant's candidature:

1. Nationality:

- For Indian Administrative Service (IAS) and Indian Police Service (IPS), the candidate must be a citizen of India.

- For other services, a candidate can be:

- A citizen of India.

- A citizen of Nepal or Bhutan.

- A Tibetan refugee who came to India before January 1, 1962, with the intention of settling in India.

- A person of Indian origin who has migrated from Pakistan, Burma, Sri Lanka, East African countries of Kenya, Uganda, the United Republic of Tanzania, Zambia, Malawi, Zaire, Ethiopia, and Vietnam intending to settle in India.

2. Age Limit:

- A candidate should be between the ages of 21 and 32 years.

- There are age relaxations for candidates belonging to SC/ST (up to 5 years), OBC (up to 3 years), and other specified categories.

3. Educational Qualification:

- A candidate must hold a bachelor's degree from a recognized university or institution.

4. Number of Attempts:

- General candidates: 6 attempts

- OBC candidates: 9 attempts

- SC/ST candidates: No limit on attempts

- Persons with Benchmark Disability: Depending on the category to which they belong, the number of attempts is defined.

Traits/Criteria that are Not Entertained:

- **Criminal History**: If a candidate has been convicted of a criminal offense and has been sentenced to imprisonment, they may face disqualification. However, minor offenses that do not result in imprisonment might not necessarily disqualify a candidate, but they have to be declared.

- **Misbehavior during Exam**: Any misbehavior during the exam or interview can lead to disqualification.

- **Providing False Information**: If it's found that a candidate has provided false information or concealed information during the application process, their candidature can be canceled.

- **Defaulting on a Government Loan**: Candidates who have defaulted on a loan from a government cooperative or financial institution are not eligible.

- **Dismissal from Previous Government Service**: If a candidate has been dismissed from any previous government service, they are usually disqualified.

Other Relevant Criteria:

- **Physical Standards**: For certain services like the IPS, there are specific physical standards and medical tests that candidates must meet.

◆ **Marital Status**: A candidate, if married and has more than one spouse living, or if a candidate marries another person while the first spouse is alive, will not be eligible to appear for the exam. This, however, does not apply to candidates belonging to communities where such marriages are customary.

In conclusion, while the UPSC has defined specific criteria for eligibility, it's essential to understand that the commission aims to recruit individuals of high moral and ethical caliber. Any discrepancies in behavior, false information, or criminal history can adversely impact an aspirant's chances. Always referring to the official UPSC notification for the year of the examination is crucial as rules and criteria might undergo changes.

POTENTIAL PITFALLS IN THE CSE JOURNEY: UNDERSTANDING DISQUALIFICATIONS AND THE UPSC'S DISCRETIONARY AUTHORITY IN SELECTION – STRATEGIES TO NAVIGATE SUCCESSFULLY

Yes, there are specific conditions where CSE aspirants can face disqualification. The UPSC has outlined these in the examination notification and related rules. Here are some conditions:

Conditions for Disqualification:

1. **Furnishing False Information**: If an aspirant provides incorrect or false information during the application process or at any stage of the examination, they can face disqualification.

2. **Misbehavior**: Any misconduct during the examination, interview, or any stage of the selection process can lead to disqualification. This includes cheating during the exam.

3. **Unfair Means**: Use of unfair means, trying to copy or take assistance in the examination, or acting in a disorderly manner can result in disqualification.

4. **Defaulting on Government Loans**: Aspirants who have defaulted on loans taken from a government cooperative bank or financial institution might be ineligible.

5. **Dismissal from Government Service**: If an aspirant has previously been in government service and was dismissed for misconduct or insubordination, it can lead to disqualification.

6. **Criminal Convictions**: If an aspirant has been convicted of a criminal offense and has served a jail term, it might lead to disqualification.

7. **Marrying while having a Living Spouse**: Marrying when one has another spouse living, except in communities where such marriages are customary, can lead to disqualification.

Discretionary Powers of UPSC:

The UPSC does have certain discretionary powers. These include:

1. **Decision on Ambiguous Cases**: In cases where there's ambiguity or if a situation isn't clearly defined in the rules, the decision of the UPSC is considered final.

2. **Medical Examination**: After the interview stage, candidates have to undergo a medical examination. The decision on medical fitness, especially for services like IPS, is discretionary based on established medical standards.

3. **Doubtful Cases**: If there's any doubt regarding the eligibility of a candidate, the decision of the UPSC is considered final.

Strategies to Overcome Potential Pitfalls:

1. **Honesty**: Always provide accurate and truthful information during the application and selection process.

2. **Awareness**: Be thoroughly aware of all the rules and regulations of the examination. Always refer to the official notification and related documents.

3. **Preparation**: Properly prepare for the examination, which reduces the chances of panic and potential misbehavior during the exam.

4. **Seek Guidance**: In case of doubts, especially related to eligibility or any other aspect of the examination, seek guidance. This can be from mentors, coaching institutes, or even directly from UPSC if needed.

5. **Maintain Integrity**: Even in situations of stress or uncertainty, always maintain personal integrity and ethical behavior.

6. **Stay Updated**: Keep track of all UPSC notifications and any changes in rules or criteria.

Factors/Causes:

1. **Financial Constraints**: Preparing for UPSC CSE can be expensive, especially if one opts for coaching. Not everyone can afford the resources or relocate to places like Delhi, which is known as a hub for UPSC preparation.

2. **Vast Syllabus**: The syllabus for CSE is vast, and the depth of understanding required is immense. This sometimes becomes overwhelming for aspirants.

3. **Lack of Proper Guidance**: Not everyone gets the right guidance or mentoring. Wrong guidance can derail the preparation.

4. **Language Barriers**: For many, English isn't the first language. While UPSC does provide options to take the exam in various languages, most of the resources, mock tests, and preparation materials are in English.

Issues:

1. **Mental Health**: The stress and pressure associated with such a competitive exam can lead to mental health challenges like anxiety, depression, or burnout.

2. **Physical Health**: Continuous studying and lack of physical activity can lead to various health issues.

3. **Social Isolation**: Many aspirants cut off from social interactions to focus on studies, leading to feelings of isolation.

4. **Peer Pressure**: Seeing peers succeed or move ahead in other professions while one is still attempting can be disheartening.

Difficulties:

1. **Staying Updated**: The dynamic nature of the syllabus, especially current affairs, requires aspirants to be continually updated with national and international happenings.

2. **Balancing Prelims & Mains Preparation**: The nature of prelims (objective) and mains (descriptive) is quite different. Balancing preparation for both can be a challenge.

3. **Selection of Optional Subject**: It's a major decision that can make or break one's chances. The wrong choice can lead to loss of interest or poor scores.

4. **Time Management**: With vast syllabus and limited time, managing time effectively becomes crucial.

5. **Handling Failures**: Not every attempt is successful. Handling failures, picking oneself up, and preparing again requires mental fortitude.

Strategies to Overcome:

1. **Well-structured Study Plan**: Having a structured study plan can help in systematically covering the syllabus.

2. **Peer Groups**: Forming or being a part of a study group can help in mutual learning and staying motivated.

3. **Mock Tests & Regular Assessments**: Taking regular tests can help in self-assessment and understanding weak areas.

4. **Staying Physically Active**: Incorporate some form of physical exercise in the routine.

5. **Mindfulness & Meditation**: To address stress and anxiety.

6. **Seeking Professional Help**: If facing severe anxiety or depression, it's crucial to seek professional help.

7. **Utilize Online Resources**: There are many online platforms, apps, and websites that offer quality content for UPSC preparation. This can be useful for those who cannot afford expensive coaching.

In summary, while the path to cracking the CSE is filled with challenges, with determination, proper planning, and the right strategies, these challenges can be overcome. Remember, the UPSC is an esteemed body that upholds the highest standards of fairness and integrity in its selection process. The key for aspirants is to be genuine, dedicated, and well-prepared, ensuring they align with the values expected of a future civil servant.

THE ROLE OF MENTORSHIP IN THE CSE JOURNEY: EVALUATING ITS NECESSITY, TIMING, AND CHOOSING THE RIGHT GUIDE – A CRITICAL INSIGHT

Absolutely, mentorship plays a pivotal role in the journey of many CSE aspirants. Here's a critical analysis of mentorship for UPSC CSE aspirants:

How:

1. **Guided Study**: A mentor can help in charting out a personalized study plan based on the strengths and weaknesses of the aspirant.

2. **Feedback Mechanism**: Regular answer writing is vital for Mains. A mentor can review and provide feedback on answer scripts.

3. **Resource Allocation**: With a plethora of materials available, a mentor can guide on what to read and what to skip.

4. **Strategy Formulation**: Forming strategies for prelims, mains, and even for the interview can be streamlined with experienced insights.

5. **Moral Support**: At times, aspirants might feel low or directionless. A mentor can provide the needed moral and emotional support.

Why:

1. **Experience**: A mentor, especially someone who has gone through the process, can offer invaluable insights from their journey.

2. **Avoid Common Pitfalls**: Many aspirants make avoidable mistakes. Having someone to guide can help in circumventing these.

3. **Structured Preparation**: Mentorship ensures that preparation is not haphazard but follows a structure.

4. **Time Efficiency**: With the right guidance, aspirants can save time, which is of the essence in UPSC preparation.

5. **Motivation**: There are times when the journey becomes tough. At such times, a word of encouragement from a mentor can make a difference.

When:

1. **Initial Phase**: When one is starting out and is unaware of the nuances of the exam.

2. **After a Failed Attempt**: To understand what went wrong and how to strategize for the next attempt.

3. **Before Mains/Interview**: For specific guidance on answer writing and personality test.

Whom:

1. **Successful Candidates**: Those who've cleared the exam and are in the services can provide firsthand insights.

2. **Experienced Teachers**: Those who have been coaching aspirants for years and have a broad perspective on the exam trends.

3. **Seniors/Peers**: Sometimes, even peers or seniors who are into preparation can act as mentors by sharing their experiences, resources, and strategies.

Critical Points:

1. **Dependency**: While mentorship is beneficial, it's essential not to become overly dependent. The aspirant must remember that the mentor is there to guide, not spoon-feed.

2. **Varied Opinions**: Sometimes, multiple mentors might have differing views. It's up to the aspirant to take a call on what advice to follow.

3. **Cost**: Professional mentorship, especially from coaching institutes, might be costly. Aspirants must weigh the benefits against the cost.

4. **Over-reliance on Past Strategies**: What worked for a mentor in the past might not necessarily work for the aspirant today, given the dynamic nature of the UPSC exam.

To conclude, while mentorship is highly beneficial, it's equally crucial for the aspirant to be proactive, adaptive, and not consider the mentor's word as the gospel truth. They should be discerning and integrate the guidance they receive into a strategy that works best for them personally.

COMMON HURDLES IN THE CSE JOURNEY AND STRATEGIES TO NAVIGATE THEM SUCCESSFULLY

Cracking the UPSC Civil Services Examination (CSE) is a challenging task, and aspirants often fall into certain pitfalls during their preparation. Let's outline these common pitfalls and strategies to overcome them:

Common Pitfalls:

1. **Lack of Structured Study Plan**: Many aspirants start their preparation without a clear study plan, leading to haphazard and ineffective learning.

2. **Over-reliance on Multiple Resources**: Aspirants sometimes gather too many study materials and books but don't get around to studying them deeply.

3. **Neglecting NCERTs**: Skipping basic NCERT books in favor of advanced materials can leave gaps in foundational knowledge.

4. **Inadequate Answer Writing Practice**: Not practicing answer writing for the Mains can hinder performance, regardless of one's knowledge.

5. **Ignoring Current Affairs**: Some aspirants focus solely on static portions, neglecting the dynamic current affairs segment.

6. **Poor Time Management**: Not allocating time efficiently for different subjects, revisions, and mock tests.

7. **Not Analyzing Previous Year Papers**: Without understanding the pattern and type of questions, aspirants might study topics irrelevant to the examination.

8. **Neglecting Health**: Continuous study without breaks can affect physical and mental health.

9. **Overconfidence or Underconfidence**: Both can be detrimental. Overconfidence might lead to lax preparation, while underconfidence can induce unnecessary anxiety.

10. **Not Being Updated with UPSC Notifications**: Missing out on any changes in the syllabus, exam pattern, or dates.

Strategies to Overcome:

1. **Structured Study Plan**: Begin with a clear, realistic, and flexible study plan. Allocate time for different subjects, revisions, and mock tests.

2. **Focused Study Materials**: Stick to a limited set of trusted resources and revise them multiple times.

3. **NCERTs First**: Start with NCERT books to build foundational knowledge before moving on to advanced materials.

4. **Regular Answer Writing**: Dedicate time daily or weekly for answer writing. Join test series or form study groups for peer reviews.

5. **Daily Current Affairs**: Dedicate some time daily for newspapers or trusted current affairs sources. Make notes for revision.

6. **Effective Time Management**: Use techniques like the Pomodoro method, setting short-term goals, and taking periodic breaks.

7. **Analyze Previous Year Papers**: This gives an understanding of the exam pattern and helps in prioritizing topics.

8. **Maintain Health**: Regular physical activity, proper diet, adequate sleep, and mindfulness practices can boost both health and productivity.

9. **Stay Balanced**: Regularly assess your preparation to avoid overconfidence. At the same time, believe in your capabilities to boost confidence.

10. **Stay Updated**: Regularly check the official UPSC website for any notifications or updates related to the examination.

Remember, while the journey of CSE preparation is long and challenging, understanding these pitfalls and actively working to avoid them can significantly enhance the chances of success.

THE IMPACT OF CONSISTENCY, EFFECTIVENESS, BALANCE, AND CURRENT AWARENESS ON THE SUCCESS RATE OF CSE ASPIRANTS

The UPSC Civil Services Examination (CSE) is one of the most challenging competitive exams in India. Given its comprehensive syllabus, evolving nature, and the sheer number of aspirants, consistency, effectiveness, balance, and staying updated are paramount. Let's delve into how the absence of each of these factors can impact the success rate of CSE aspirants:

1. **Inconsistency:**
   - **Impact**: Inconsistency leads to irregular study patterns, resulting in an uneven coverage of the syllabus. As the syllabus is vast, a lack of regularity can mean that large portions remain untouched or inadequately prepared.
   - **Result**: Reduced chances of clearing the prelims due to incomplete knowledge, and even if one clears, inadequate depth in subjects can be a hindrance in mains and interview.

2. **Ineffectiveness:**
   - **Impact**: Merely studying for long hours without a strategy or understanding doesn't yield results. Ineffectiveness can result from not revising, not practicing answer writing, or not understanding key concepts.
   - **Result**: Aspirants might find themselves unable to recall or apply what they've learned in the actual examination, leading to poor performance.

3. **Lack of Balance:**
   - **Impact**: It's not just about academic preparation. Lack of balance can mean neglecting physical health, mental well-being, or other essential

areas like current affairs or optional subjects. Over-stressing one area can lead to burnout or gaps in another.

♦ **Result**: A lack of holistic preparation, which the CSE demands. Physical or mental burnout can severely affect performance on the examination day or even during the entire preparation phase.

4. Not Staying Updated:

♦ **Impact**: The CSE, especially in its Prelims and General Studies papers, often features current affairs and recent developments. Not staying updated can mean missing out on these areas. Additionally, UPSC might introduce changes in syllabus, pattern, or other aspects.

♦ **Result**: Aspirants might find unexpected questions in the exam or miss out on critical information about the examination itself. This can lead to loss of marks and even failure to meet the cut-off.

In essence, the success rate in the CSE is a combination of knowledge, strategy, and well-being. Missing out on consistency, effectiveness, balance, and updates can significantly dent an aspirant's chances of success. Given the intense competition, where even a single mark can make a difference, these factors become all the more crucial.

Navigating Societal Expectations: Challenges Faced by CSE Aspirants:

CSE aspirants, particularly in a country like India where the UPSC examination is held in high regard, often grapple with various societal pressures. Here are some of the most common societal pressures they face:

1. High Expectations:

♦ Many families regard the CSE as the pinnacle of academic and professional achievement. This can put a heavy burden on aspirants, as they are expected to live up to these standards.

2. Comparison with Peers:

♦ Friends or relatives who clear the exam or achieve other significant milestones in life can become unintentional benchmarks, leading to incessant comparisons.

3. **Age and Marriage:**

   ♦ In many parts of India, there's an expectation to marry at a certain age. Aspirants, especially women, often face pressure to get married and settle down, which can conflict with their CSE preparations.

4. **Economic Pressure:**

   ♦ Preparing for CSE can be a long journey, often requiring years. Aspirants might face economic pressures, especially if they are not working and have to rely on their families or savings.

5. **Comments and Judgments:**

   ♦ If an aspirant doesn't succeed in initial attempts, they might face unsolicited advice, comments, or even direct judgments from relatives, neighbors, and sometimes even strangers.

6. **Alternative Career Paths:**

   ♦ Pressure to consider alternative, more "stable" career paths after "giving enough time" to CSE preparations can be a source of stress.

7. **Mental Health Stigma:**

   ♦ The immense pressure can take a toll on an aspirant's mental health. However, seeking psychological help or counseling might be stigmatized, making it harder for aspirants to address their mental health concerns.

8. **Gender Biases:**

   ♦ Female aspirants might face gender-specific pressures, including biases against women in certain services or roles or expectations related to household responsibilities.

9. **Community and Social Standing:**

   ♦ In certain communities, becoming a civil servant is seen as elevating the family's social status. This can add an additional layer of pressure on aspirants.

10. Time Pressure:

- As the number of attempts and age limit for CSE are capped, aspirants often feel the ticking clock, with society reminding them of the "limited attempts" they have.

It's essential for aspirants to develop coping mechanisms, seek support systems, and, if necessary, professional counseling to manage and navigate these societal pressures effectively.

RISING ABOVE PEER COMPARISONS: STRATEGIES FOR CSE PREPARATION SUCCESS

Comparison with peers can be a significant source of stress for CSE aspirants, but it's essential to remember that each individual's journey is unique. Here are some strategies to overcome the pressure of peer comparison:

1. **Self-awareness**: Recognize that comparing oneself with others is a natural human tendency but is not always productive. Awareness is the first step toward change.

2. **Individual Journey**: Understand that everyone's journey is unique. Some might take longer to achieve their goals, while others might have different paths entirely. Embrace your personal journey.

3. **Limit Social Media**: Social media platforms often present a filtered view of reality. If you find yourself constantly comparing your progress with peers on these platforms, consider taking a break or limiting your usage.

4. **Set Personal Milestones**: Instead of measuring your success against others, set personal goals and milestones. Celebrate your achievements, no matter how small.

5. **Stay Focused**: Remember your reason for undertaking the CSE journey. Revisiting your motivation can help anchor you when peer comparisons distract you.

6. **Open Communication**: Talk to friends or peers about your feelings. Chances are, they too feel the pressure. Sharing your concerns can be cathartic and offer a fresh perspective.

7. **Positive Affirmations**: Reinforce positive self-talk. Whenever you find yourself making negative comparisons, counteract them with positive affirmations about your progress and abilities.

8. **Seek Mentorship**: A mentor, especially someone who has been through the CSE process, can offer guidance, reassurance, and a broader perspective.

Their experiences can provide valuable insights into managing comparison pressures.

9. **Mindfulness and Meditation**: Engaging in mindfulness practices and meditation can help ground you and reduce anxiety stemming from comparisons. It helps in staying present and focused on one's own path.

10. **Avoid Competitive Study Groups**: If you're in a study group where there's more competition than cooperation, consider finding a new group or studying alone. The environment should foster collaboration and mutual growth.

11. **Counseling**: If peer comparison is affecting your mental well-being, consider seeking counseling or therapy. Professional guidance can provide coping strategies and a fresh perspective.

Remember, the CSE journey is a marathon, not a sprint. Everyone has their pace, strengths, and challenges. Stay true to your path, and trust that with perseverance, you'll reach your destination.

The Sacrifices Behind UPSC Preparation: A CSE Aspirant's Journey:

Yes, CSE aspirants often make numerous sacrifices during their UPSC preparation, given the demanding nature of the examination process. Here's a breakdown of some common sacrifices:

1. **Personal Time**: With the vast syllabus, aspirants often sacrifice personal downtime, dedicating most of their day to studying.

2. **Social Life**: Social gatherings, outings, and casual hangouts often take a backseat. This might mean missing out on family functions, weddings, or even small get-togethers with friends.

3. **Career Opportunities**: Some aspirants leave lucrative job offers or even quit their existing jobs to focus solely on UPSC preparation.

4. **Financial Independence**: Resigning from jobs for preparation might mean giving up a steady source of income. This might lead to financial dependence on family or savings, at least temporarily.

5. **Hobbies**: Many aspirants sideline their hobbies, whether it's reading non-academic books, playing musical instruments, or pursuing sports.

6. **Health**: The long study hours can lead to irregular sleep patterns, unhealthy eating habits, and a lack of physical activity.

7. **Relationships**: UPSC preparation can strain relationships. Aspirants might have less time for their partners, family, and friends, which can sometimes lead to misunderstandings.

8. **Mental Well-being**: The pressure of the exam, coupled with the sacrifices, can sometimes take a toll on one's mental health.

9. **Immediate Gratification**: Instead of enjoying current pleasures like vacations, shopping, etc., aspirants often have a long-term vision, hoping their sacrifices will pay off when they clear the exam.

10. **Physical Relocation**: Many aspirants move to cities like Delhi, known for its UPSC coaching infrastructure, leaving behind their homes and comfort zones.

11. **Postgraduate Plans**: Some students delay or give up plans for post-graduation, research, or any other higher studies abroad to focus on UPSC.

Despite these sacrifices, many aspirants find the process worth it, considering the potential rewards – serving the nation, achieving job security, gaining respect in society, and the numerous opportunities that civil services in India offer. It's essential, however, for aspirants to maintain a balance and ensure they aren't neglecting their health or well-being entirely.

NAVIGATING THE HURDLES: OVERCOMING CHALLENGES IN CSE PREPARATION

Certainly, preparing for the Civil Services Examination (CSE) conducted by the UPSC is a daunting task. Here are some common challenges faced by aspirants and suggestions to overcome them:

1. **Vast Syllabus:**
   - **Challenge**: The CSE syllabus is extensive, covering subjects from history to science to current affairs.
   - **Solution**: Break down the syllabus into manageable parts and create a realistic timetable. Stick to a few standard books for each subject instead of gathering a lot of material.

2. **Information Overload:**
   - **Challenge**: With the plethora of study materials, coaching classes, and online resources, it's easy to get overwhelmed.
   - **Solution**: Choose your resources wisely. Stick to a few trusted sources and revise them multiple times.

3. **Balancing Prelims and Mains Preparation:**
   - **Challenge**: Prelims require factual knowledge, while Mains demand analytical skills.
   - **Solution**: Integrate the preparation for both. For instance, when studying a topic, gather facts for Prelims and understand its analytical aspect for Mains.

4. **Time Management:**
   - **Challenge**: Finding enough time to cover the entire syllabus and revise.
   - **Solution**: Prioritize topics based on previous years' questions. Use techniques like the Pomodoro Technique for efficient studying.

5. Handling Pressure and Stress:

- **Challenge**: The intense competition and the stakes involved can be stressful.

- **Solution**: Meditation, physical exercise, and short breaks can help manage stress. It's crucial to maintain a work-life balance.

6. Financial Constraints:

- **Challenge**: Enrolling in coaching institutes, buying study materials can be expensive.

- **Solution**: Use free online resources, borrow books, or buy second-hand. Remember, expensive coaching isn't mandatory to clear CSE.

7. Staying Updated with Current Affairs:

- **Challenge**: The dynamic nature of the UPSC exam requires aspirants to be updated with current events.

- **Solution**: Regularly read newspapers, follow a few trusted websites, and make notes on relevant issues.

8. Avoiding Procrastination:

- **Challenge**: Postponing studies and being inconsistent.

- **Solution**: Set short-term goals, reward yourself upon completion, and stay disciplined.

9. Choosing the Right Optional Subject:

- **Challenge**: With many subjects available, choosing the right one can be tough.

- **Solution**: Consider your interest in the subject, available resources, and scoring trends.

10. Societal and Peer Pressure:

- **Challenge**: Handling expectations and comparisons.

- **Solution**: Stay focused on your goal, avoid negative influences, and seek support from like-minded individuals or groups.

11. Dealing with Failure:

- ◆ **Challenge**: Not clearing in the first attempt can be disheartening.

- ◆ **Solution**: Take failures as learning experiences. Analyze mistakes, rectify them, and come back stronger.

Preparation for the CSE requires perseverance, patience, and consistent hard work. It's essential to believe in oneself, stay updated, practice regularly, and most importantly, maintain a positive mindset throughout the journey.

CSE DREAMS AMIDST CONTROVERSIES: ADDRESSING PERCEIVED INJUSTICES AND UPSC'S INTERVENTIONS

The Civil Services Examination (CSE) conducted by the Union Public Service Commission (UPSC) is one of the most prestigious and toughest exams in India. Over the years, aspirants have raised concerns and grievances about various aspects of the examination. Here are some areas where candidates have felt unfair treatment or unjust exam practices:

1. **Ambiguity in Questions**: There have been instances when candidates have pointed out that certain questions in the prelims or mains had more than one correct answer or were ambiguously framed.

2. **Evaluation Concerns**: Some candidates have expressed doubts over the subjective nature of the evaluation in the Mains examination, especially for the essay and optional papers.

3. **Syllabus and Question Pattern Changes**: UPSC has, in the past, made changes to the syllabus or the pattern of questions. Such changes can be challenging for aspirants who have been preparing based on the old pattern.

4. **Language Bias**: Candidates from regional language backgrounds occasionally express that there is a bias towards English and Hindi medium students, especially in the interview process.

5. **Age and Attempt Limit**: There's been a recurring demand to increase the age limit and the number of attempts, especially after any major changes in the exam pattern or syllabus.

6. **Issues with Admit Cards or Centres**: Some candidates have faced issues like not receiving admit cards on time or being allocated exam centers far from their hometowns.

Interventions by UPSC and the Central Government:

1. **Transparent Answer Keys**: UPSC releases the answer keys for the preliminary examination, which allows candidates to assess their performance and challenge ambiguous or incorrect questions.

2. **Redressal Mechanism**: Candidates can submit representations against any question they find incorrect or ambiguous within a specified time after the prelims.

3. **Compensatory Extra Attempts**: When the UPSC introduced the CSAT (Civil Services Aptitude Test) in 2011, many aspirants felt it was biased against students from humanities backgrounds. In response, the government provided compensatory extra attempts to candidates.

4. **Feedback Mechanism**: UPSC has a feedback mechanism in place. Based on feedback and expert review, changes have been made in the past, like revising the syllabus in 2013.

5. **Language Policy Revisions**: UPSC has made changes to the language policies over the years. Aspirants are allowed to take the exam in any of the languages listed in the Eighth Schedule of the Indian Constitution.

6. **Legal Route**: In several cases, candidates have approached the courts with their grievances. Depending on the merit of the case, the courts have given directives to the UPSC or the government.

The UPSC and the Central Government, over the years, have tried to make the CSE process as transparent and just as possible. However, given the scale of the examination and the stakes involved, grievances and demands for change are expected. It's essential for aspirants to stay updated with the UPSC notifications and adapt to the changes while ensuring they voice genuine concerns through the appropriate channels.

CENTRAL GOVERNMENT AND PARLIAMENTARY INFLUENCE ON CSE: A COMPREHENSIVE ANALYSIS OF IMPACT AND TAKEAWAYS

The Civil Services Examination (CSE) conducted by the Union Public Service Commission (UPSC) is a testament to India's central government and parliamentary system's functioning. The recruitment through CSE shapes the administrative machinery that assists in implementing the policies of the elected government.

Influence of Central Government and Parliamentary System on CSE:

1. **Mandate and Independence**: The UPSC operates with a mandate from the Constitution of India. The autonomy ensures that the selection process remains impartial, independent, and free from political interference.

2. **Policy Implementation**: The elected central government's policies are implemented by the officers recruited through CSE. The officers play a significant role in translating the parliamentary decisions into on-ground actions.

3. **Representative of Diversity**: Just as the parliamentary system ensures representation from various parts of the country, the CSE also aims at selecting candidates from diverse backgrounds. There's a reservation system in place to ensure that various social groups are adequately represented.

4. **Feedback Mechanism**: Civil servants act as a bridge between the public and the government. They provide ground-level feedback to the policymakers, ensuring the policies are more in line with the real-world scenarios.

Takeaways:

1. **Reflects Democratic Ethos**: The transparent and competitive nature of CSE reflects the democratic ethos of India's parliamentary system. It

ensures that individuals from diverse backgrounds get an opportunity to be part of the administration.

2. **Adaptability**: Over the years, UPSC has shown adaptability by revising the syllabus, changing exam patterns, and incorporating current issues, much like the adaptability our parliamentary system shows to the changing aspirations of its people.

3. **Accountability**: Just as elected representatives are accountable to the public, civil servants are accountable to the public and the elected representatives. This hierarchy ensures the implementation of policies as envisioned by the elected government.

4. **Training and Orientation**: Once recruited, the civil servants undergo extensive training to understand the country's administrative machinery, its parliamentary system, the Constitution, and other aspects that are crucial for their roles.

5. **Role of Ethics and Integrity**: Both the parliamentary system and the CSE emphasize ethics and integrity. While elected representatives are expected to maintain a certain standard, the civil servants, too, are trained to ensure they uphold the highest ethical standards.

Critiques:

1. **Perceived Political Influence**: Over the years, there have been allegations that civil servants sometimes act under political pressure. However, the CSE training emphasizes neutrality and commitment to the Constitution.

2. **Evolving Challenges**: The challenges faced by the nation are ever-evolving. Some critics argue that the CSE syllabus or training might not be entirely in sync with the contemporary challenges. However, UPSC has shown a trend of updating its syllabus and training modules.

In conclusion, the CSE is deeply interwoven with the central government and the parliamentary system. The examination's primary purpose is to recruit individuals who would be the pillars of the country's administrative machinery, ensuring the smooth functioning of the government's policies and decisions. The CSE's evolving nature, coupled with its foundational principles, ensures that it stays relevant and continues to attract some of the brightest minds in the country.

CONSTITUTIONAL AMENDMENTS AND THEIR IMPACT ON UPSC CSE SELECTION PATTERNS: AN EVOLUTIONARY OVERVIEW

The Union Public Service Commission (UPSC), which conducts the Civil Services Examination (CSE), derives its powers and functions directly from the Constitution of India. Specifically, Article 315 to 323 of the Constitution pertains to the UPSC. However, the specifics of the CSE pattern, syllabus, and processes are administrative in nature and do not necessitate constitutional amendments. Instead, such decisions fall under the purview of the UPSC's administrative discretion, in consultation with the Government of India.

Throughout the history of the CSE, there have been several changes to the examination's structure, pattern, and syllabus. Still, most of these changes have been administrative decisions rather than outcomes of constitutional amendments.

However, the Constitution has been amended several times to address matters related to public employment, including reservations. Some of these amendments indirectly influence the selection process in the CSE:

1. **42nd Amendment, 1976**: Added clauses (4A) and (4B) to Article 16. This allowed the state to make provisions for reservation in promotions for Scheduled Castes and Scheduled Tribes. This can indirectly affect the service conditions of those selected through the CSE.

2. **77th Amendment, 1995**: Inserted clause (4A) to Article 16 to enable reservation in promotions for SCs and STs.

3. **81st Amendment, 2000**: Added clause (4B) to Article 16, permitting the state to consider unfilled reserved vacancies of a year as a separate class of vacancies to be filled up in succeeding years. This can indirectly affect the number of available vacancies in a given year for CSE.

4. **82nd Amendment, 2000**: Inserted a provision in Article 335 to allow the state to make any provision in favor of the members of SCs and STs for relaxation in qualifying marks in any examination or lowering the standards of evaluation. While UPSC has maintained its standards, this amendment provides constitutional backing for potential relaxations.

5. **85th Amendment, 2001**: Changed the wording of Article 16(4A) to benefit SC/ST employees in matters of promotion.

6. **117th Amendment, 2012 (not passed)**: Aimed to provide reservations in promotions for SC/ST candidates without affecting the administration's efficiency.

It should be noted that while the above constitutional amendments pertain to public employment and can indirectly influence CSE, they don't directly change the CSE's structure or pattern. Those decisions are typically administrative and are made by UPSC in consultation with the government, based on evolving needs and feedback.

"A Historical Analysis of UPSC-CSE Reforms: Yearly Modifications, Impacts, and Outcomes:"

It's challenging to list every modification made to the UPSC-CSE historically as the examination has undergone numerous changes over the years. However, I can provide a table highlighting some of the major changes that have been instituted over time:

Year	Modification	Impact	Advantages	Disadvantages	Awareness
1979	Introduction of the CSAT (Civil Services Aptitude Test)	Introduced objective-type papers, reducing subjectivity	Provided a level playing field, ensured a broader test of aptitude	Reduced the weight of domain-specific knowledge	High, led to coaching centers emphasizing on CSAT preparation

Year	Modification	Impact	Advantages	Disadvantages	Awareness
2011	Changes in Prelims pattern (two objective type papers)	Shift from a single General Studies paper and an optional subject to two objective type papers - one on General Studies and one on aptitude	More equitable for all aspirants regardless of their educational background	Some concerns regarding the CSAT being biased against humanities and language students	Widely discussed and debated; led to changes in preparation strategies
2013	Changes in Mains pattern (four General Studies papers)	Reduction in optional subjects for the Mains from two to one	Encouraged a more comprehensive understanding of various subjects	Increased the syllabus for General Studies	Significant, aspirants had to adapt to new study techniques
2015	Introduction of questions on ethics, integrity, and aptitude	Focus on moral and ethical dimensions of decision-making in the service	Ensured aspirants were evaluated on moral and ethical dimensions, not just academic knowledge	Increased the syllabus, a subjective area of evaluation	High; initiated discussions on moral and ethical dimensions of governance
2020 (Due to COVID-19)	Reduced number of exam centers and adherence to safety protocols	Logistical and safety challenges, especially for aspirants from remote areas	Ensured the safety of aspirants during the pandemic	Difficulties in travel and logistics for some aspirants	High; led to discussions on accessibility and fairness

This table provides an overview of some of the significant changes. The advantages and disadvantages are based on feedback from aspirants and stakeholders, and might not represent a universal perspective.

MASTERING THE CSE MAINS: TECHNIQUES, TRAITS, AND COMPREHENSIVE STRATEGIES FOR SUCCESS

Preparing for the UPSC Civil Services Mains Examination requires a combination of dedication, strategy, and consistency. Here's a comprehensive guide to help aspirants prepare for the CSE Mains:

I. Understanding the Exam Pattern

The Mains consists of:

- 9 theory papers: 2 qualifying papers (One of an Indian Language and English), 4 General Studies papers, 1 Essay paper, 2 Optional Subject papers.

2. Start with the Syllabus

- Download the official syllabus.

- Break it into micro-topics to ensure no topic is left unattended.

3. Integrated Approach with Prelims

- While the Prelims are more fact-oriented, the Mains are analytical. But a lot of content overlaps. An integrated approach helps to streamline preparation.

4. Focus on Answer Writing

- Practice is key. Join a test series or form a group to evaluate each other's answers.

- The Mains exam is as much about content as it is about presentation. Structure your answers well with introductions, body, and conclusions.

- Stick to word limits.

5. Master the Art of Essay Writing

♦ Choose topics you are comfortable with.

♦ Practice writing essays and get them evaluated. Structure your essays with a clear introduction, body, and conclusion.

6. Optimal Selection of Optional Subject

♦ Choose a subject you have interest in, and resources for. The subject should also have good scoring potential.

♦ Past question papers can give an insight into the type of questions asked.

7. Revision

♦ Regular revision is crucial. One round of study is never enough.

♦ Make short notes for quick revisions.

8. Current Affairs

♦ Regularly follow newspapers like The Hindu, Indian Express, and magazines like Yojana, Kurukshetra.

♦ Make notes on current issues and their various dimensions.

9. Enhance Writing Speed

♦ Mains require you to write long answers within a limited time frame. Regular practice can enhance your writing speed.

10. Stay Updated with Reports

♦ Important reports by bodies like NITI Aayog, Finance Commission, Law Commission, etc., should be referred to.

11. Seek Guidance

♦ If possible, join coaching institutes for guidance, especially for the optional subject and answer writing.

♦ Online platforms also offer quality guidance and resources.

12. Stay Motivated

♦ Remember why you started. Stay connected with peers who motivate you. Read toppers' interviews for insights and motivation.

13. Health is Wealth

- Regular breaks, a balanced diet, and proper sleep are crucial.

- Meditation can help in maintaining focus.

14. Utilize Technology

- Websites, apps, online classes, and YouTube channels can provide valuable resources and tips.

15. Mock Tests

- Regular mock tests will get you in the habit of writing for long hours and help you manage time better.

16. Feedback System

- Regularly get your answers evaluated by mentors, peers, or through online platforms.

17. Stay Ethical

- The paper on Ethics, Integrity, and Aptitude requires an understanding of ethical issues and case studies. Understand the concepts and practice case studies.

Traits Required for Cracking CSE Mains:

- **Determination and Consistency:** The preparation phase can be long and requires you to be consistent.

- **Analytical Abilities:** Mains answers require analysis more than mere facts.

- **Time Management:** Balancing different subjects and ensuring regular revisions.

- **Resilience:** It's a tough journey, and resilience ensures you keep going despite setbacks.

Remember, while guidance and resources are necessary, ultimately, it's the aspirant's personal drive, commitment, and strategy that make the difference.

DECIPHERING THE CSE MAINS EXAM PATTERN: COMMON MISTAKES AND HOW TO AVOID THEM

Understanding the pattern of the UPSC Civil Services Mains examination is crucial for its preparation. It's not just about knowing the subjects but about comprehending the depth, breadth, and nature of questions. Here's how to best understand the pattern and the common pitfalls:

Best Ways to Understand the CSE Mains Exam Pattern:

1. **Official UPSC Syllabus:** Always begin with the official UPSC Mains syllabus, available on the UPSC website. It's detailed and provides a clear framework of what's expected from an aspirant.

2. **Previous Year Question Papers:** Analyze the last 5-10 years' question papers. They give you the best insight into the pattern, type of questions, and the recurring themes.

3. **Toppers' Insights:** Many successful candidates share their strategies, experiences, and insights about the Mains pattern in interviews, blogs, or videos. This helps in understanding the intricacies of the exam.

4. **Mock Tests:** Enrolling in mock test series gives you a real-time experience of the examination. It also helps identify areas of improvement.

5. **Coaching Institutes' Material:** While not always necessary, some reputed coaching institutes provide material and insights that break down the syllabus and pattern in an easy-to-understand manner.

6. **Online Platforms and Forums:** Websites, discussion groups, and forums such as Unacademy, Insights on India, and IASBaba can provide insights into the Mains pattern.

Pitfalls in Understanding the CSE Mains Exam Pattern:

1. **Over-reliance on Coaching Institutes:** While coaching can be beneficial, believing solely in their methods and not developing one's own understanding can be detrimental.

2. **Not Practicing Answer Writing:** Knowing the pattern is one thing, but practicing it is equally important. Without regular answer writing, aspirants often find themselves unable to finish the paper on time.

3. **Neglecting Some Papers:** Often, aspirants spend more time on subjects they find tough and neglect areas they feel confident in, leading to unbalanced preparation.

4. **Not Updating with Current Affairs:** Many neglect the dynamic part of the syllabus, thinking static portions will suffice. However, UPSC focuses a lot on the current applicability of static knowledge.

5. **Ignoring the Basics:** Some aspirants delve too deep into advanced books without clearing basics from NCERTs, leading to a shaky foundation.

6. **Not Revising:** Many aspirants cover the syllabus but forget to revise, which is a grave mistake given the vastness of the Mains syllabus.

7. **Misinterpreting Syllabus:** Instead of understanding the topics, some aspirants take the syllabus too literally and don't explore around topics mentioned.

Remember, while the CSE Mains pattern provides a structure, it's the nuanced understanding of its demand and consistent practice that will enable an aspirant to perform effectively.

Yes, there are official materials recommended for UPSC CSE Mains aspirants which primarily come from the government and its bodies. These are essential readings as they provide authentic information that can be quoted in the exam and are valued by the examiners. Here's a list of these materials:

1. **NCERT Textbooks:** While these are basics for the Prelims, they remain indispensable for the Mains as well. Textbooks from Class 6 to 12, especially in History, Geography, Political Science, and Economics, lay a foundational understanding.

2. **Economic Survey:** Released annually by the Ministry of Finance, it gives a comprehensive overview of India's economic progress, challenges, and policy directions.

3. **Annual Budget:** Highlights from the Union Budget give insights into the government's fiscal policies, priorities, and economic forecasts.

4. **Yojana & Kurukshetra Magazines:** Published by the Publications Division of the Government of India, these monthly magazines cover developmental and welfare initiatives, policies, and socio-economic issues.

5. **Reports of NITI Aayog:** They provide data, insights, and policy directions on various developmental aspects of the country.

6. **India Year Book:** Published by the Publications Division, it's an annual book detailing India's progress in various fields, from rural to urban, science to culture, and economy to defense.

7. **Reports of Ministry of Environment, Forest, and Climate Change:** Especially relevant for topics related to environmental conservation, pollution, climate change, etc.

8. **Government Websites:** Websites of various ministries (like Ministry of Health and Family Welfare, Ministry of Rural Development, etc.) provide white papers, notifications, policies, and schemes which are helpful.

9. **ARC Reports:** The reports of the Administrative Reforms Commission give a comprehensive idea about governance reforms.

10. **Census Data:** Provides statistical data on population, literacy, and various other demographic details.

11. **Selected documents and reports from international bodies:** While not "official" from the Indian government's perspective, reports and findings from organizations like the World Bank, IMF, UNDP, WTO, and WHO are valuable, especially for GS Paper II (International Relations) and GS Paper III (Economics).

12. **Gazette Notifications:** Issued by the Government of India, these provide information on new policies, amendments, and reforms.

13. **Five Year Plans:** Although NITI Aayog has taken over the planning process, the old Five Year Plans contain vast data and strategies that can be relevant for some topics.

14. **PRS Legislative Research:** An initiative that provides updates on the latest bills, legislative briefs, and the status of various laws.

15. **Rajya Sabha TV Programs:** Shows like 'The Big Picture', 'India's World', and 'Science Monitor' give an in-depth analysis of current issues.

16. **Speeches by Key Dignitaries:** Speeches made by the President of India, the Prime Minister, RBI Governor, etc., during official events, often lay down the vision and policy directions.

17. **Publications of RBI:** For topics related to banking, monetary policies, economic trends, etc., reports and bulletins issued by the Reserve Bank of India are invaluable.

18. **Sachar Committee Report:** Important for topics related to minorities in India.

19. **Justice Verma Committee Report:** Important for issues related to women's safety and legal reforms.

20. **Law Commission Reports:** Provide insights into legal reforms and issues related to the judiciary.

21. **2nd ARC Reports:** (Apart from the earlier mention) - These are comprehensive reviews on various aspects of administration and governance.

22. **Manorama Yearbook:** Contains a summary of events, trends, and updates on various fields.

23. **PIB (Press Information Bureau) Updates:** Official news updates and releases by the Government of India.

24. **IGNOU Study Material:** Sometimes, the study material from Indira Gandhi National Open University (IGNOU) can be beneficial, especially for topics like Society in India, Public Administration, etc.

25. **Economic Survey and Budget:** Annual documents presented by the Ministry of Finance. They provide comprehensive details about the Indian economy and government's fiscal policies.

26. **Annual Reports:** Issued by various ministries. They detail the initiatives, achievements, and future strategies of the respective ministries.

27. **Yojana and Kurukshetra Magazines:** Monthly publications by the Government of India that cover various socio-economic issues.

28. **Down To Earth Magazine:** Provides insights into environmental and ecological issues, both national and global.

29. **The Hindu Centre for Politics and Public Policy:** Offers policy reports, research papers, and perspectives on various subjects.

30. **EPW (Economic and Political Weekly):** Provides profound analyses of current socio-economic and political issues.

31. **World Bank and IMF Reports:** Especially useful for topics related to the economy, development, and global economic trends.

32. **India Yearbook:** Published by the Publication Division, it's a comprehensive digest of India's progress in different fields.

33. **IDSA (Institute for Defence Studies and Analyses):** Reports, analyses, and perspectives on defense and international relations topics.

34. **Government Websites:** Websites like India.gov.in, data.gov.in provide vast amounts of data and information on various topics.

35. **Think Tank Publications:** Organizations like Observer Research Foundation (ORF), Centre for Policy Research (CPR), and Brookings India publish reports and analyses on various topics relevant for the UPSC exams.

36. **Environment and Ecology:** Websites of WWF, IUCN, UNEP, and the Ministry of Environment, Forest and Climate Change can offer valuable information.

37. **UN Reports:** On topics like Human Development, Climate Change, Gender, and more.

38. **LexisNexis's** Bare Acts for Law Optional: If one has law as an optional, the up-to-date bare acts and commentaries are vital.

39. **Drishti IAS and Vision IAS Monthly Magazines:** They provide monthly compilations of important news tailored for UPSC aspirants.

40. **Mrunal.org:** For economy and various other topics presented in an easy-to-understand format.

41. **BYJU's Free IAS Prep:** Offers daily news analysis, topic-wise curated articles, and more.

42. **PIB (Press Information Bureau):** The official portal for government's communication. Offers press releases about government decisions, policies, and updates.

43. **PRS Legislative:** Offers briefs on bills and acts introduced and passed in the Parliament.

44. **IASbaba:** A platform that provides various resources like daily current affairs, monthly magazines, and specific topic analysis.

45. **Insights on India:** Known for its daily answer writing challenges and in-depth articles on various topics.

46. **RSTV and LSTV:** 'Rajya Sabha TV' and 'Lok Sabha TV' debates and discussions, especially 'The Big Picture', are very helpful in understanding different perspectives on current issues.

47. **AIR News Analysis:** All India Radio's daily news analysis provides a neutral perspective on important events.

48. **NCERT Textbooks:** Especially for history, geography, science, and economics, NCERT books are the backbone. They provide foundational knowledge.

49. **ClearIAS:** Provides mock tests, study materials, toppers' interviews, and strategies.

50. **Unacademy:** Many educators provide free courses, and there are also paid courses for in-depth preparation.

51. **CivilsDaily:** Known for its easy-to-read daily news snippets and monthly compilations.

52. **Gktoday:** Useful for its daily current affairs, quizzes, and a series of articles on general studies topics.

53. **The Print, The Wire, Livemint:** For diversified opinions on current issues. However, aspirants should develop the acumen to filter out biased views.

54. **EPW Engage:** Provides detailed articles on diverse topics, very helpful for essay papers and in enhancing answer quality.

55. **ForumIAS:** Apart from the content, the portal also has an active community of aspirants. This aids in doubt-clearance and sharing of resources.

56. **IAS Parliament:** Provides a lot of free content, including daily current affairs, monthly compilations, and 'Shankar IAS' environment notes.

57. **Google Scholar:** If an aspirant needs to delve deep into a topic, especially for the optional paper or essay.

58. **YouTube Channels:** 'Study IQ Education', 'Only IAS', 'Neostencil' and more, have content-rich videos on varied subjects.

59. **JSTOR:** For those who have humanities as their optional, this digital library can be of great help.

60. **Oxford's Very Short Introductions:** For almost any topic, these books provide concise yet comprehensive insights.

61. **Telegram Channels:** Various channels and groups exist that provide daily news summaries, PDFs of magazines, and mock questions. However, aspirants must ensure that these channels are legitimate and the content is reliable.

It's essential to note that one doesn't need to read these documents cover to cover. What's crucial is understanding the core ideas, data points, and policy recommendations. Also, remember to update the latest versions of these documents, especially the Economic Survey and the Budget, every year. While all these sources provide rich and valuable information, it's essential for aspirants to use them judiciously. The UPSC syllabus is vast, but not everything under the sun is asked. The idea is to integrate knowledge from these sources with the demands of the syllabus and previous year's question papers to have a balanced and effective preparation.

It's essential to note that aspirants don't need to go through all these resources exhaustively. Depending on the topics they're covering and the areas they feel they need more information on, they can selectively opt for these resources. The main idea is to stay updated, make comprehensive notes, and regularly revise. Remember, quality always trumps quantity in UPSC preparation.

Remember, the UPSC exam is vast, but the key is not to get lost in the ocean of materials. Aspirants should choose a few, reliable sources and stick to them, revising regularly. Too many sources can lead to confusion and information overload. It's about studying smart, not just hard.

INTEGRATING PRELIMS, MAINS, AND PERSONAL INTERVIEW PREPARATION: STRATEGIES FOR CSE ASPIRANTS

The personal interview, also known as the Personality Test, is the final hurdle in the UPSC CSE examination process. The board assesses not just the intellectual qualities of the candidate, but also social and leadership attributes. Here's how to prepare for it:

1. **Self-awareness:**
   - Begin with understanding yourself. Know your strengths, weaknesses, hobbies, and interests.
   - Expect detailed questions from your DAF (Detailed Application Form), especially regarding your background, work experience, hobbies, and optional subject.

2. **Current Affairs:**
   - Remain updated with the latest events and news, both nationally and internationally.
   - Your opinion on current issues might be asked. Be prepared with a balanced viewpoint.

3. **Depth of Subject Knowledge:**
   - Revise your optional subjects since questions could be asked from there.
   - If you have academic or work experience in specific fields, be prepared to answer questions related to those.

4. **Mock Interviews:**
   - Enroll in a mock interview series provided by various coaching institutions. This helps you get feedback and rectify errors.

- Group mock interviews with peers can also be helpful.

5. Communication Skills:

- Your ability to articulate your thoughts clearly is essential.

- Regular discussions on topics with friends or peer groups can enhance this.

6. Soft Skills:

- Good manners, a friendly disposition, and a calm demeanor can leave a lasting impression.

- Develop listening skills. Wait for the interviewer to finish before you respond.

7. Practice Situational Questions:

- Be prepared for hypothetical situations and case studies, especially if they relate to the role of a civil servant.

8. Stay Healthy:

- Mental and physical well-being is crucial. Regular exercise, meditation, and a balanced diet can help keep stress at bay.

9. Feedback and Adaptability:

- Use feedback from mock interviews constructively. Adapt and make changes to your approach if needed.

10. Stay Positive:

- Confidence is key. Trust your preparation and stay optimistic.

11. Integration with Prelims and Mains:

- Remember key points from your mains answers; you can use these in your interview.

- Link current affairs (from prelims preparation) with issues you have written about in mains.

- Revise the ethical concepts and examples you've prepared for the Ethics paper (GS-IV) as they can be a base for many behavioral questions.

12. Environment and Ecology:

- Given its contemporary relevance, be prepared for issues related to climate change, sustainable development, and other environmental concerns.

13. Revisit Graduation Subject:

- If your graduation subject is different from your optional, be ready to answer questions on it as interviewers often probe here.

14. Dress Appropriately:

- Wear formal attire. It shouldn't be flashy but should make you look and feel confident.

15. Keep Answers Non-Controversial:

- While it's important to have an opinion, ensure it's a balanced one. Avoid making extreme or potentially controversial statements.

1. Behavioral Consistency:

- If you've expressed an opinion in the written mains examination, ensure you can defend it if questioned during the interview.

2. Body Language:

- While content matters, non-verbal communication can also send strong signals. Maintain good posture, avoid fidgeting, and establish appropriate eye contact.

3. Understanding the UPSC Mandate:

- Revisit the UPSC's mandate for the interview, which emphasizes assessing the candidate's suitability for a career in public service.

4. Language Proficiency:

- Even though you can choose the medium of communication, ensure you're clear and articulate in whichever language you choose.

5. Handling Stressful Situations:

- Be prepared for stress interview tactics where interviewers might play devil's advocate or counter your opinions. Remain calm and stick to your reasoned arguments.

6. Ethical Dilemmas:

- Brush up on ethical frameworks and be ready to apply them to real-world situations or dilemmas the panel might present.

7. Hobbies and Extracurriculars:

- Be genuine about your hobbies. If you mention reading, be prepared to discuss the last few books you've read. Similarly, if you mention a sport, you might be asked about recent developments or rules of that sport.

8. Service Preference:

- Have a well-thought-out reason for your cadre and service preference. It shows clarity of purpose.

9. Location-Specific Questions:

- If you belong to a specific state or region, brush up on significant historical, geographical, and contemporary issues related to that region.

10. International Affairs:

- With India's rising global profile, be well versed in the nation's foreign policy, especially concerning our neighbors and major global powers.

11. Analyze Previous Years' Transcripts:

- Go through toppers' interview transcripts or videos, if available. This gives you an insight into the nature of questions asked and the depth sought by the board.

12. Cultural Awareness:

- You might get questions related to India's diverse cultural heritage, including art forms, dances, and festivals.

13. Have a Constructed Worldview:

- Beyond facts, it's essential to have a worldview. For instance, what's your take on democracy, secularism, socialism, etc., in the Indian context?

14. Mock Panel with Diverse Backgrounds:

- If you're attending mock interviews, try to have them with panels from varied backgrounds. This will expose you to a broader set of questions and viewpoints.

15. Prepare a Good Introduction:

- "Tell me about yourself" or similar questions are commonly asked. Have a concise, structured, and engaging self-introduction ready.

Remember, the interview is not just about knowledge but about your personality as a whole. The board assesses whether you are suitable for a career in the civil services. It's an opportunity to show your character, judgment, and suitability for the demands of the job.

Lastly, always remember the UPSC interview is more of a conversation than an interrogation. The panel is genuinely interested in understanding your personality, clarity of thought, and your passion for public service. Being authentic and true to oneself is crucial.

DYNAMICS OF THE CSE PERSONAL INTERVIEW: PANELS, COMPOSITION, LOCATIONS, AND TRANSPARENCY INSIGHTS

The UPSC Civil Services Examination (CSE) personal interview, often referred to as the Personality Test, is the final phase in the selection process. Here's a detailed breakdown of the process and its intricacies:

1. **Number of Panels:**

   - There are multiple panels conducting interviews simultaneously on any given day of the UPSC interviews. The exact number might vary each year, but typically there are around 5-6 panels functioning.

2. **Composition of the Panel:**

   - Each panel comprises 4-5 members. One of them is the chairman of the board, and the others are members. These members are either part of the UPSC or are invited experts from various fields.

3. **Venue:**

   - The interviews are conducted at the UPSC office in New Delhi.

4. **Transparency:**

   - The UPSC has a reputation for maintaining a fair and transparent process throughout all stages of the examination. The interview is no exception. The objective is to assess the personality and suitability of the candidate for a career in public service. Panelists are trained to be neutral and unbiased.

   - However, the exact marking criteria and deliberations about the candidate post-interview remain confidential.

5. **Stages and Dynamics:**

   - While the interview appears as a continuous conversation, there are usually underlying stages:

- ◆ **Introduction**: Often starts with a general question, like asking the candidate to introduce themselves.

- ◆ **DIP Analysis**: DIP stands for Detailed Application Form, which every candidate fills before the interview. Questions can revolve around hobbies, work experience, places of residence, educational institutions, etc.

- ◆ **Current Affairs**: As an aspiring civil servant, candidates are expected to be aware of national and international happenings.

- ◆ **Subjective Questions**: These could be related to the candidate's graduation subject, optional subject in mains, or any other topic the panel deems important.

- ◆ **Situational or Hypothetical Questions**: Aimed at gauging the moral compass, decision-making ability, and clarity of thought of the candidate.

- ◆ **Conclusion**: The panel may end with a light question or simply a remark.

6. Dimensions:

- ◆ While knowledge is tested, the primary focus remains on personality traits - honesty, integrity, clarity of thought, decision-making ability, and the potential for leadership.

- ◆ Communication skills, presence of mind, and the ability to handle stress are other dimensions assessed during the interview.

7. Duration:

- ◆ Typically, an interview can last between 20-35 minutes. However, there's no fixed time, and duration doesn't necessarily correlate with the outcome.

It's essential for aspirants to remember that the panel has vast experience and can easily identify pretentious answers. Authenticity, humility, and clarity are always appreciated.

Historical Analysis of CSE Personal Interview Questions: Key Insights for Aspirants:

Certainly! While I don't have access to a real-time database of questions, I can provide insights based on historical trends and widely-shared experiences of candidates over the years. The UPSC interview is quite dynamic, and while no two interviews are the same, some common themes and areas often come up.

Here's an analysis based on historical patterns:

1. **Background-centric Questions:**
   - **Education**: Questions based on the subject of graduation, post-graduation, or any other significant qualifications.

   - **Work Experience**: If a candidate has worked or is working, questions related to their job profile, challenges faced, industry trends, etc., can be asked.

   - **Home State/District**: About the socio-economic challenges, cultural significance, history, or any current event related to the aspirant's hometown or state.

2. **Hobbies & Interests:**
   - This is a favorite area for many board members. It's advisable for candidates to be well-prepared on their stated hobbies.

   - Questions can range from basics (e.g., "Why do you like this hobby?") to more in-depth discussions.

3. **Opinion-based Questions:**
   - Questions that gauge your stand on contentious topics, such as women's reservation, capital punishment, electoral reforms, etc.

   - Here, logical reasoning, respect for diverse opinions, and balanced arguments are valued more than the stand itself.

4. **Hypothetical Situational Questions:**
   - These questions are designed to test decision-making skills, ethical considerations, and on-the-spot thinking.

5. Current Affairs:

- Issues of national and international importance. Candidates are often asked about their views on recent happenings.

6. Service Preference & Role of Civil Services:

- Why do you want to join civil services?

- Why have you placed a particular service (IAS/IPS/IFS etc.) as your top preference?

7. Questions on Optional Subject:

- Can range from basic concepts to its application in real-life administration.

Key Takeaways for CSE-Aspirants:

1. **Authenticity**: Always be genuine in your responses. If you don't know an answer, it's okay to admit it.

2. **Stay Updated**: Regularly read newspapers and be aware of the latest happenings around the world, especially events that have a significant societal or policy impact.

3. **Revise Basics**: Especially regarding your graduation subject, optional subject, and work profile (if applicable).

4. **Clarity of Thought**: It's essential not just to know but to be able to articulate your thoughts succinctly and clearly.

5. **Mental Calmness**: It's not just what you say but how you say it. Stay calm, even if provoked or presented with a challenging scenario.

6. **Ethics & Integrity**: Always opt for the ethical stand, especially in situational questions. The board values honesty and integrity.

7. **Practice**: While real UPSC interviews are unpredictable, practicing mock interviews can help in building confidence and refining presentation skills.

8. **Dress Appropriately**: Wear formal attire. It reflects professionalism and shows respect for the institution and the process.

9. **Politeness & Respect**: Always greet the board members when you enter and exit the interview room. Remember to thank them after the interview.

10. **Listen Carefully**: Before answering, ensure you've understood the question. Don't rush. Take a moment to gather your thoughts if needed.

11. **Body Language**: Maintain an upright posture and avoid fidgeting. Maintain eye contact with the board member who's asking the question.

12. **Stay Neutral**: When discussing sensitive or controversial topics, it's wise to provide a balanced perspective rather than taking an extreme stand unless you're absolutely sure about your stance and can defend it adequately.

13. **Prepare Personal Questions**: Be prepared for questions like:

    1. Why civil services after engineering/medicine/Ph.D. etc.?

    2. Gap years or attempts: What did you do during this time?

    3. Why did you choose your particular optional subject?

14. **Stay Updated with DAF**: The Detailed Application Form (DAF) you submit has a lot of information about you. Review it carefully. Anything you've mentioned can be a starting point for questions.

15. **Learn to Gracefully Navigate Questions**: If you don't know the answer to a question, don't bluff. It's better to politely say that you don't recall or are not sure about the specific detail.

16. **Take Feedback but Don't Overanalyze**: If you're attending mock interviews, take feedback constructively. However, remember that every interview is different. Don't overanalyze or get bogged down by any negative feedback.

17. **Stay Healthy**: Ensure you're getting enough rest and are mentally and physically fit before the interview. This helps in keeping stress levels in check.

18. **Have a Positive Attitude**: Consider the interview as a discussion rather than an interrogation. The panel is more interested in understanding your thought process rather than checking if every answer is correct.

19. **Real-life Situational Judgement**: Sometimes, questions might be framed around recent events you might have witnessed or your personal experiences. Be prepared to share and analyze them.

20. **Continuous Learning**: Even after your mains examination, continue the habit of daily newspaper reading and staying updated with current affairs.

Remember, the interview is about your personality, not just knowledge. The board wants to understand you as a person and gauge if you're suitable for a career in the civil services. It's an opportunity to have a meaningful discussion with some of the most experienced individuals in the bureaucracy. Approaching it with curiosity and a learning mindset can make the process enriching.

Remember, the UPSC interview panel has decades of experience. Their primary aim is to assess if you are suited for the administrative roles you're aspiring for. So, show them your best self, be authentic, and trust your preparation. Every candidate's journey is unique, and the key is to remain persistent and learn continuously.

ESSENTIAL SOFT SKILLS AND CORE COMPETENCIES FOR CSE ASPIRANTS: A PATH TO SUCCESS

Certainly, cracking the Civil Services Examination (CSE) demands more than just academic knowledge. Aspirants need a mix of soft skills and other capabilities to not only clear the examination but also to excel in their roles once they're in service. Here are some of the essential skills and traits:

1. **Communication Skills:**

   - **Written Communication:** Crucial for Mains where clarity, conciseness, and coherence in answers can fetch higher marks.

   - **Verbal Communication:** Vital for the interview round. The ability to express oneself clearly and logically is sought after.

2. **Analytical and Critical Thinking:** The ability to analyze vast amounts of information, discern patterns, and think critically is crucial for both Prelims and Mains.

3. **Time Management:** With the vast syllabus, managing one's preparation time effectively is essential. This also applies to the exam setting, especially for Prelims, where time is limited.

4. **Empathy and Compassion:** Given that a career post-CSE involves public service, an empathetic and compassionate approach is invaluable. This is often assessed during the interview.

5. **Decision Making:** Future civil servants are often put in situations requiring quick and effective decision-making. Having a decisive nature can be an asset.

6. **Stress Management and Resilience:** The CSE preparation journey is long and demanding. The ability to manage stress, bounce back from setbacks, and remain resilient is vital.

7. **Leadership Qualities**: These are especially important for roles that involve leading teams, like that of an IAS or IPS officer.

8. **Interpersonal Skills**: Building rapport with the community, peers, and subordinates is essential for administrative roles.

9. **Ethical Integrity**: Maintaining a strong ethical compass is paramount, especially given the responsibilities and powers of the roles aspirants will take on.

10. **Negotiation Skills**: Especially important for officers in roles where negotiation, be it with community stakeholders or inter-departmentally, is a regular part of the job.

11. **Adaptability and Flexibility**: Civil servants are often posted in varied regions, facing different challenges. Being adaptable is crucial.

12. **Self-awareness**: Knowing one's strengths, weaknesses, biases, and areas of improvement can be a great asset during preparation and service.

13. **Reading Comprehension**: A significant part of Prelims and even some portions of Mains requires candidates to quickly comprehend and analyze given texts.

14. **Public Speaking**: While not directly tested in CSE, as administrators, officers often have to address gatherings, conduct meetings, or give press briefings.

15. **Problem-solving Skills**: This involves both analytical skills and creativity, as officers might face unprecedented situations requiring innovative solutions.

16. **Cultural Awareness**: Given the diversity of India, understanding various cultures, languages, and traditions can be very beneficial.

17. **Networking**: Building a support system with fellow aspirants and mentors can aid the preparation journey.

18. **Research Skills**: Especially during Mains, aspirants should be adept at researching various topics effectively.

Developing these skills is a continuous process and not just restricted to the duration of CSE preparation. Many of these skills are life skills that will aid aspirants in various stages and roles of their lives.

"Historical Analysis: Academic Backgrounds of Successful CSE Candidates and Their Unique Traits:"

The Civil Services Examination (CSE) in India has seen successful candidates from a diverse array of academic backgrounds. Over the years, this diversity has led to a rich tapestry of officers with varied skill sets and perspectives, which greatly benefit the administrative framework of the country. Let's delve into a historical analysis of the academic backgrounds of successful CSE candidates and the unique traits they bring:

1. **Humanities and Social Sciences:**
   - Historical Trend: Traditionally, a significant number of successful candidates come from humanities backgrounds, especially subjects like History, Political Science, Geography, and Public Administration.

   - Unique Traits:

   - Contextual Understanding: Their training provides them with a contextual understanding of society, its challenges, and the nuances of governance.

   - Empathy and People-Centric Approach: Having studied subjects related to human societies, they often display a heightened sense of empathy.

2. **Engineering:**
   - Historical Trend: In recent decades, with the rise of engineering education in India, there's been a notable increase in engineers cracking the CSE.

   - Unique Traits:

   - Problem Solving: Engineers tend to have a methodical approach to problem-solving, stemming from their technical background.

   - Tech-Savviness: In an era of e-governance and technological solutions, this background can be advantageous.

3. **Medicine:**
   - Historical Trend: Medical doctors, though fewer in number compared to engineers and humanities graduates, have consistently made their mark in CSE results.

- Unique Traits:

- Patient Care and Compassion: Dealing with patients nurtures empathy and compassion, vital traits for public servants.

- Scientific Acumen: Their methodical and scientific approach to problems can be a boon in administration.

4. Sciences:

- Historical Trend: Candidates with a pure science background, including Physics, Chemistry, Biology, and Mathematics, have been consistent, if not dominant, in the CSE arena.

- Unique Traits:

- Analytical Mindset: A science background instills a logical and analytical mindset.

- Research-Oriented: A knack for research and evidence-based conclusions is a trait often found in science graduates.

5. Commerce and Management:

- Historical Trend: Commerce graduates and MBAs have also been part of the successful candidates' list, though they might not be as numerous as engineers or humanities graduates.

- Unique Traits:

- Financial Acumen: Their grasp over economic and financial matters can be highly beneficial.

- Management Skills: Organizational and management skills are often sharpened in this academic background.

6. Law:

- Historical Trend: Law graduates have been consistently making it to the civil services, with some even securing top ranks.

- Unique Traits:

- Legal Acumen: Their deep understanding of laws and the legal system is a direct advantage in administrative roles.

- Rhetorical Skills: Trained in debates and arguments, they often possess strong communication skills.

Conclusion:

The diversity of academic backgrounds among successful CSE candidates reflects the multifaceted nature of the examination and the roles it leads to. Each background brings its unique strengths, making the Indian administrative framework a blend of varied skills and perspectives. The CSE does not favor any specific academic background but rewards a deep understanding of subjects, a keen sense of current affairs, and the ability to apply knowledge in real-world scenarios.

NAVIGATING CSE CHALLENGES: FROM ASPIRANT HURDLES TO POST-SELECTION REALITIES AND THE LONGEVITY OF PREPARATORY LESSONS

The journey of a Civil Services Examination (CSE) aspirant is one marked by numerous challenges, not only during the preparatory phase but also in the post-selection landscape of administrative roles. Here's a comprehensive look at navigating these challenges:

1. **Aspirant Hurdles:**

    ◆ **Vast Syllabus**: The sheer breadth of the UPSC syllabus can be daunting. From history to science and technology, the range of topics is vast.

    ◆ **Information Overload**: With a plethora of resources available, distinguishing between essential and non-essential material is crucial.

    ◆ **Mental Pressure**: The multiple attempts, high competition, and societal expectations can take a toll on mental health.

Strategies:

    ◆ **Structured Study**: Breaking down the syllabus and setting a timetable helps in systematic preparation.

    ◆ **Seek Guidance**: Connecting with mentors or joining study groups can provide direction.

    ◆ **Mindfulness and Stress Management**: Regular breaks, meditation, and hobbies can help maintain mental equilibrium.

2. **Post-Selection Realities:**

    ◆ **Administrative Challenges**: New officers often confront a series of challenges such as handling bureaucracy, managing local politics, and navigating the vast governmental machinery.

- **Ethical Dilemmas**: Situations may arise where one's moral compass is tested. Navigating these with integrity is essential.

- **Balancing Personal and Professional Life**: The demanding job can sometimes overshadow personal commitments and aspirations.

Strategies:

- **Networking**: Building relationships with peers, seniors, and locals can be beneficial.

- **Continuous Learning**: The CSE preparation is just the beginning. Officers should be prepared for lifelong learning.

- **Work-Life Balance**: Setting boundaries, delegating tasks, and effective time management can help.

3. Longevity of Preparatory Lessons:

- **Interdisciplinary Approach**: The vast syllabus ensures officers have basic knowledge across multiple disciplines, assisting in multifaceted decision-making.

- **Analytical Skills**: The nature of the exam fosters a candidate's analytical and critical thinking abilities, proving useful in bureaucratic roles.

- **Endurance**: The prolonged and intense preparation phase inculcates endurance, patience, and perseverance – qualities that stand officers in good stead throughout their careers.

Strategies:

- **Application of Knowledge**: Translating bookish knowledge into ground-level execution is the real test of an officer's mettle.

- **Continuous Revision**: While the foundational knowledge remains, refreshing and updating one's information is crucial given the dynamic nature of administrative roles.

- **Seek Feedback**: Regular introspection and feedback from peers and the public can be instrumental in an officer's growth.

Conclusion:

The journey from a CSE aspirant to an officer is a transformative one. While the preparation phase throws its own set of challenges, the post-selection landscape is filled with real-world dilemmas and opportunities. The lessons learned during preparation aren't limited to cracking the exam but extend to navigating the vast expanse of Indian bureaucracy effectively and ethically.

DOES SOCIETY, ECONOMY, RELIGION, AND CASTE INFLUENCE SUCCESS IN THE CIVIL SERVICES EXAMINATION?

The Civil Services Examination (CSE) in India is designed to be a merit-based test that selects candidates for various administrative roles in the Indian government. However, the broader socio-economic, religious, and caste contexts can't be completely isolated from the equation. Below are some insights into how these factors may influence success in the CSE:

Societal Factors:

1. **Social Support and Expectations**: In many cases, familial and societal expectations can serve as motivators but can also add pressure.

2. **Peer Influence**: The society one is a part of may either encourage or discourage the aspiration to become a civil servant, affecting mental preparation.

3. **Gender Roles**: Prevalent gender roles and stereotypes in certain societies may also affect an individual's choice to pursue or not pursue CSE.

Economic Factors:

1. **Resource Allocation**: From books to coaching classes, preparing for the CSE can be expensive. Economic background, therefore, can be a significant factor.

2. **Opportunity Cost**: Those from economically disadvantaged backgrounds may not have the luxury of dedicating extended periods solely to preparation.

Religious Factors:

1. **Cultural Capital**: Different communities have varying levels of access to educational resources and social networks, which can play an indirect role in preparation.

2. **Religious Holidays and Rituals**: These may either serve as small breaks boosting mental health or can be potential distractions depending upon one's level of religious involvement.

Caste Factors:

1. **Reservation System**: India's reservation policy aims to provide better opportunities to historically marginalized communities, impacting the competition dynamics.

2. **Social Discrimination**: Experiencing discrimination based on caste can be demoralizing and impact an aspirant's performance negatively.

Mitigation Factors:

1. **Online Resources**: The internet is increasingly leveling the playing field by providing access to quality resources irrespective of one's background.

2. **Government Schemes**: Scholarships, free coaching, and other schemes are made available to those from disadvantaged backgrounds.

3. **Diverse Exam Panel**: UPSC takes great care to ensure that the interview panel is diverse, limiting the impact of personal biases.

While these factors can influence an aspirant's journey, they do not definitively determine success or failure in the CSE. The CSE remains a largely merit-based exam, and aspirants from all backgrounds have been known to succeed through dedicated preparation, effective strategy, and hard work.

WHICH GENDER HAS HISTORICALLY ACHIEVED GREATER SUCCESS IN THE CIVIL SERVICES EXAMINATION?

As of my last updates, there is no definitive or comprehensive data to suggest that one gender has historically achieved greater success in the Civil Services Examination (CSE) conducted by the Union Public Service Commission (UPSC) in India. While the examination is designed to be gender-neutral and merit-based, societal factors can sometimes influence the composition of candidates at both the application and selection stages.

Observations:

1. Increasing Female Representation: Over the years, there has been a gradual increase in the number of female candidates applying for and clearing the CSE. Successful female candidates have gone on to hold high-ranking positions in the bureaucracy.

2. Changing Trends: While earlier batches may have seen a male-dominated cohort, this has been changing. More recently, women have been topping the exams and getting into premier services like IAS, IPS, and IFS.

3. Barriers to Entry: Societal expectations and gender roles may have acted as barriers for women in the past, but the situation is evolving. Initiatives aimed at encouraging women to participate in civil services are making a difference.

4. Meritocracy: Since the CSE is a merit-based exam, gender should theoretically have no influence on the outcome. However, societal, educational, and economic factors can indirectly influence the rate of success among genders.

5. Diverse Roles: While some services within the civil services might see a gender skew due to the nature of the job, overall, the UPSC aims to maintain a balanced ratio.

6. Transparency: The UPSC is known for its transparent and unbiased examination process, which minimizes the scope for any gender-based discrimination.

7. Notable Women in Service: Over the years, women like Kiran Bedi, Meera Borwankar, and Smita Sabharwal, among others, have made significant contributions to public service, serving as role models for future generations of women.

While both men and women have had their share of challenges and successes in the CSE, it would be misleading to claim that one gender has historically outperformed the other in a definitive manner. The trends are complex, influenced by a multitude of factors ranging from societal attitudes to educational opportunities, and they are continually evolving.

HOW DO CIVIL SERVICE ASPIRATIONS AND ECONOMIC DEVELOPMENT INTERSECT? THE ROLE OF CIVIL SERVANTS IN RESTRUCTURING THE NATION

The relationship between civil service aspirations and economic development is deeply interwoven, and understanding this intersection offers valuable insights into both individual goals and broader national objectives. Civil servants play a critical role in shaping the trajectory of a country's economic, social, and political landscape. Here's a look at some of the ways in which the aspirations to join the civil services and the nation's economic development intersect:

Driving Economic Policy:

Civil servants often occupy key positions where they can influence economic policy. From tax collection and management of public funds to the implementation of development programs, they play a pivotal role in driving economic growth.

Ensuring Governance and Stability:

Effective governance, provided by a competent civil service, is essential for a conducive economic environment. Civil servants maintain law and order, enforce contracts, and create a stable environment, all of which are prerequisites for economic development.

Resource Allocation:

One of the most direct ways civil servants influence economic development is through the allocation of state resources. They decide which sectors should be prioritized for development, balancing immediate needs against long-term sustainability.

Regulation:

Civil servants are often responsible for regulating industries, protecting consumers, and ensuring fair competition, thereby creating a more stable and competitive economic landscape.

Implementation:

Conceptualizing policy is one thing, but the real impact comes from effective implementation, usually a task relegated to the civil service. Their effectiveness in this role can significantly influence economic development.

Social Equity:

Civil servants also strive to ensure that the fruits of economic development are equitably distributed. This includes creating and implementing policies that promote social welfare, healthcare, and education, which in turn support economic growth by creating a more capable and healthy workforce.

Attracting Investment:

A transparent and efficient civil service can make a country more attractive to foreign and domestic investment, thereby spurring economic development.

Inspiring Young Talent:

The aspirational value of civil services often attracts some of the brightest minds in the country. These individuals bring their talent and energy into the public sector, potentially leading to more effective governance and, by extension, economic growth.

Restructuring the Nation:

The role of civil servants in restructuring the nation is monumental. They are the arms of the government, implementing changes and reforms that shape the future of the country. Economic restructuring, diversification, and modernization often start as policies but take life in the hands of civil servants who implement them.

The Aspirational Cycle:

As the country develops economically, educational and societal structures improve, leading to a more competent pool of civil service aspirants. This creates a virtuous cycle where better governance leads to economic development, which in turn produces better civil servants.

In conclusion, civil service aspirations are not just individual career goals; they are closely aligned with broader visions of economic development and national restructuring. As future policy-makers, administrators, and regulators, civil servants are not just symbols of individual achievement but are key players in the nation's journey towards economic and social prosperity.

WHAT ARE THE COMMON CONCERNS AND CRITICISMS AMONG CIVIL SERVICES EXAM ASPIRANTS?

The Civil Services Examination (CSE) in India is one of the most competitive and challenging exams, attracting hundreds of thousands of aspirants every year. While the exam opens doors to prestigious career paths in the public sector, it is not without its share of criticisms and concerns among aspirants. Here are some of the common issues raised:

Length and Complexity of the Examination Process

1. **Long Duration**: The entire process, from prelims to the final interview, can span over a year, which can be mentally and emotionally exhausting.

2. **Vast Syllabus**: The extensive syllabus covers a wide array of subjects, making it challenging to master all areas.

Transparency and Evaluation

1. **Subjective Scoring**: The mains and interview stages are often criticized for their subjectivity, leading to doubts about the transparency of the evaluation process.

2. **Optional Subjects**: The weightage given to optional subjects in mains can create imbalances in scores, as some subjects are perceived to be scored more leniently than others.

Socio-Economic Factors

1. **Cost of Preparation**: The high cost of coaching classes, study material, and living expenses in cities can be prohibitive for aspirants from lower socio-economic backgrounds.

2. **Rural-Urban Divide**: Aspirants from rural areas may lack access to quality coaching and study materials, putting them at a disadvantage.

Reservation and Quota System

1. **Caste-based Reservations**: The reservation system is often a point of contention, with debates on both its necessity for social justice and its impact on meritocracy.

2. **Age and Attempt Relaxations**: Similar to reservations, age and attempt relaxations for certain categories are viewed by some as diluting the competition.

Political and Bureaucratic Influence

1. **Political Influence**: There is a perception that political considerations can influence postings and career progression, leading to skepticism about the system's fairness.

2. **Corruption**: Although the UPSC is generally regarded as clean, there are concerns about corruption in state-level Public Service Commissions.

Mental Health Concerns

1. **Stress and Anxiety**: The high level of competition and the stakes involved can lead to significant stress and mental health issues.

2. **Social Pressure**: There is immense societal pressure to succeed, which can exacerbate stress and impact self-esteem.

Gender Concerns

1. **Gender Bias**: Although the number of female candidates clearing the exam has been increasing, some feel that the interview process and later job postings can be biased.

Miscellaneous

1. **Outdated Syllabus**: Critics argue that the syllabus and exam pattern need to be more aligned with contemporary issues.

2. **Lack of Practical Assessment**: The exam is mostly academic and lacks components that assess practical administrative skills.

Understanding these concerns and criticisms can offer valuable insights into areas for improvement in the examination process and help align it more closely with the aspirants' expectations and societal needs.

DO CIVIL SERVICES EXAM QUESTIONS EXTEND BEYOND THE SYLLABUS, OR ARE THEY ALL-ENCOMPASSING?

The Civil Services Examination (CSE) conducted by India's Union Public Service Commission (UPSC) has a fairly well-defined syllabus, available in the official notifications and guidelines. However, the nature of the examination is such that it tests not just rote knowledge but also the ability to analyze, interpret, and provide reasoned arguments. This means that while the questions usually fall within the scope of the syllabus, the context in which they are framed could require insights or understanding that extend beyond textbook knowledge.

Understanding the Dimensions

1. **Current Affairs**: Though the syllabus outlines broad subjects, it can't detail every issue within those subjects that could be relevant at the time of the exam. Current affairs, especially, can introduce questions that, while technically within the scope of the syllabus, require knowledge of events, policies, or perspectives that have emerged after the syllabus was published.

2. **Interdisciplinary Approach**: Some questions may require knowledge that intersects multiple disciplines. While each subject might be part of the syllabus, the question could be framed in such a way that it requires integrating information across subjects.

3. **Conceptual Understanding**: The syllabus might list a topic in a few words, but the depth of understanding required can be immense. For instance, a subject like "Indian Polity" can include questions on constitutional amendments, recent Supreme Court judgments, or the implications of new legislation, which might not be explicitly mentioned in the syllabus.

4. **Analytical Skills**: Questions, especially in the mains examination and the interview, often seek to test the candidate's ability to analyze issues

critically. This requires a nuanced understanding that goes beyond the written syllabus.

Conclusion

So, while the UPSC generally adheres to the syllabus it provides, the examination is designed to test a candidate's overall awareness, intellectual skills, and analytical abilities. As such, aspirants often find that effective preparation extends beyond simply covering the topics listed in the syllabus and involves a more comprehensive and updated understanding of issues.

DOES AN INTERDISCIPLINARY APPROACH TO STUDY AID IN SUCCESSFULLY CLEARING THE CIVIL SERVICES EXAM?

The Civil Services Examination (CSE) conducted by India's Union Public Service Commission (UPSC) is known for its broad and comprehensive syllabus that spans multiple disciplines. Given the multifaceted nature of the roles that civil servants are expected to take on, the exam seeks to assess not just subject-specific knowledge but also an aspirant's ability to integrate and apply that knowledge in complex, real-world scenarios. Therefore, an interdisciplinary approach can offer several advantages for those aiming to successfully clear the CSE.

Advantages of an Interdisciplinary Approach

1. **Broadens Perspective**: A multidisciplinary approach helps you understand issues from various angles—social, political, economic, and more. This broad perspective is beneficial for both the Preliminary and the Mains exams, where questions often require a nuanced understanding.

2. **Enhances Analytical Skills**: Looking at a subject from multiple viewpoints enhances your ability to analyze issues more critically and to see the interconnections between seemingly unrelated topics. This is especially useful for essay papers and the interview, where you are expected to present well-rounded arguments.

3. **Better Handling of Case Studies**: The Mains examination often includes case studies in the General Studies papers that require a balanced understanding of ethics, laws, and societal implications. An interdisciplinary approach prepares you to tackle these effectively.

4. **Improves Answer Quality**: A well-rounded understanding allows you to incorporate varied points into your answers, making them more comprehensive and thereby helping you score better. For example, a

question on climate change can be addressed more holistically if you understand not just the science but also the economic, social, and political dimensions of the issue.

5. **Aids in the Interview**: During the personal interview, questions can span a wide array of topics, from your optional subject to current affairs and even hypothetical situational queries that test your decision-making skills. An interdisciplinary approach ensures that you're better equipped to handle whatever comes your way.

6. **Real-world Application**: Civil servants often have to work on complex projects that involve multiple sectors such as healthcare, infrastructure, and education. An interdisciplinary approach in studies can thus mirror the kind of complexities you might face in your professional role.

Conclusion

In summary, an interdisciplinary approach can be incredibly beneficial for CSE aspirants. It not only equips them to perform well across the diverse set of papers and interviews they will face but also prepares them for the multifaceted roles they may assume as civil servants. Therefore, while specialized knowledge is important, integrating that with a broader, more interdisciplinary understanding could be the key to success in the CSE.

HOW AND WHY DO INDIVIDUALS SELECTED THROUGH THE CIVIL SERVICES EXAM CONTRIBUTE TO SHAPING MODERN INDIA? ELABORATE IN DETAIL

Individuals selected through the Civil Services Examination (CSE) in India occupy pivotal roles in the administration and governance of the country. Often considered the backbone of the Indian state, these civil servants play a multifaceted role in shaping modern India. Here's how and why they are instrumental in this regard:

Policy Formulation

1. **Influence on Policy**: Civil servants often work closely with elected officials to draft policies. Their insights and subject-matter expertise can have a significant influence on the content and direction of these policies.

2. **Research & Data Analysis**: They are also involved in researching and analyzing data to inform policy decisions, ensuring that policies are evidence-based.

Implementation of Laws and Policies

1. **Ground-Level Execution**: Civil servants are responsible for the execution of laws and policies. They ensure that the benefits of various welfare schemes reach the intended beneficiaries.

2. **Monitoring & Feedback**: They are also crucial in monitoring the implementation and providing feedback for any necessary revisions.

Social Welfare

1. **Upliftment of Marginalized Sections**: Civil servants often work towards the welfare of marginalized communities, ensuring that government programs targeting social upliftment are effectively implemented.

2. **Education & Health**: In sectors like education and healthcare, the implementation of policies by civil servants can shape societal structures for generations to come.

Economic Development

1. **Resource Allocation**: From deciding budgets to prioritizing projects, civil servants play a key role in the economic development of a region or the country at large.

2. **Attracting Investments**: Senior civil servants often engage in diplomatic and trade missions to attract foreign investment, which can be a significant economic driver.

Public Accountability

1. **Transparency**: Through efforts like Right to Information (RTI), civil servants ensure that the government's workings are transparent.

2. **Grievance Redressal**: Various mechanisms are often put in place by civil servants to hear and address the grievances of the public.

1. **Internal Security**: Civil servants in the police and administrative services play an essential role in maintaining law and order.

2. **Border Security**: Those in services like the Indian Foreign Service (IFS) play a role in shaping foreign policy, which has a direct bearing on national security.

Why Their Role is Crucial

1. **Continuity**: Unlike politicians, who may be in office for relatively short periods, civil servants often serve for decades, providing continuity in governance.

2. **Expertise**: Given the rigorous selection process and subsequent training, civil servants bring a high level of expertise to their roles.

3. **Political Neutrality**: Ideally, civil servants are politically neutral, making them trustworthy stewards of public interest.

4. **Social Impact**: Finally, the influence of civil servants extends beyond mere implementation of laws. Their role in shaping policies and public programs can have far-reaching social implications, shaping the very fabric of modern India.

In summary, civil servants are integral to both the functioning of the Indian state and the well-being of its citizens. Through their varied roles, they shape the modern nation in ways both immediate and enduring.

WHAT IS THE HIERARCHY AMONG INDIVIDUALS SELECTED THROUGH THE CIVIL SERVICES EXAM?

The hierarchy among individuals selected through the Civil Services Examination (CSE) in India varies depending on the service they are recruited into. The three major All India Services are the Indian Administrative Service (IAS), Indian Police Service (IPS), and Indian Forest Service (IFoS). There are also several other Central Services like the Indian Revenue Service (IRS), Indian Foreign Service (IFS), and others. Here's a generalized hierarchy for some of these services:

Indian Administrative Service (IAS)

1. **Sub-Divisional Officer / Sub-Divisional Magistrate (SDO/SDM)**

2. **Additional District Magistrate (ADM)**

3. **District Magistrate/District Collector**

4. **Divisional Commissioner**

5. **Secretary to the State Government**

6. **Principal Secretary to the State Government**

7. **Chief Secretary of the State**

8. **Secretary to the Government of India**

9. **Additional Secretary to the Government of India**

10. **Special Secretary to the Government of India**

11. **Cabinet Secretary to the Government of India (highest bureaucratic post in India)**

Indian Police Service (IPS)

1. **Assistant Superintendent of Police (ASP)**

2. **Superintendent of Police (SP)**

3. **Senior Superintendent of Police (SSP)**

4. **Deputy Inspector General of Police (DIG)**

5. **Inspector General of Police (IG)**

6. **Additional Director General of Police (ADG)**

7. **Director-General of Police (DGP)**

Indian Foreign Service (IFS)

1. **Third Secretary**

2. **Second Secretary**

3. **First Secretary**

4. **Counselor**

5. **Minister**

6. **Ambassador or High Commissioner**

Indian Revenue Service (IRS)

1. **Assistant Commissioner of Income Tax/Customs**

2. **Deputy Commissioner of Income Tax/Customs**

3. **Joint Commissioner of Income Tax/Customs**

4. **Additional Commissioner of Income Tax/Customs**

5. **Commissioner of Income Tax/Customs**

6. **Principal Commissioner of Income Tax/Customs**

7. **Chief Commissioner of Income Tax/Customs**

8. **Principal Chief Commissioner of Income Tax/Customs**

Note: This is a generalized hierarchy and the nomenclature or the sequence may vary depending on the state or the specific rules of the service. Also, there are other central services each with their own hierarchical structure.

These officers can also be deputed to central government jobs at various stages of their careers, and many hold critical positions in central agencies, ministries, public sector undertakings, and more.

IS THE CIVIL SERVICES EXAM SELECTION PROCESS INFLUENCED BY HIGH-RANKING OFFICERS AND POLITICIANS? A CRITICAL EXAMINATION

The Civil Services Examination (CSE) in India is conducted by the Union Public Service Commission (UPSC), an autonomous constitutional body. The UPSC operates under strict guidelines and is known for maintaining a high level of integrity and impartiality in its examination processes. However, like any complex system, the CSE has its own set of criticisms and concerns regarding its operations. Below is a critical examination of whether the CSE selection process is influenced by high-ranking officers and politicians.

Legal and Constitutional Framework

The UPSC and the CSE are governed by a stringent legal and constitutional framework aimed at ensuring fairness, transparency, and equality of opportunity for all aspirants. The constitutional status of the UPSC provides it a level of autonomy that insulates it from undue political or bureaucratic influence.

Mechanisms for Transparency

The UPSC employs multiple layers of anonymity and checks to ensure the evaluation process is impartial. From the initial application to the final interview, processes are designed to minimize any scope for bias or influence. For example, the answer sheets for the written exams are often coded to ensure anonymity, and interview panels are carefully selected to reduce potential bias.

Public Perception and Controversies

Despite these measures, there have been occasional allegations and rumors about the influence of politicians or high-ranking officers. However, such allegations have rarely been substantiated. Public perception may sometimes carry notions of partiality, but there is generally a lack of evidence to support such claims.

Role of Media and Civil Society

Media and civil society organizations keep a close watch on the UPSC's activities. Any credible allegations of corruption or undue influence would likely attract significant public scrutiny, adding another layer of accountability.

Potential Areas of Concern

While the exam process itself is rigorously designed to prevent influence, there are external factors like coaching availability, educational background, and socio-economic conditions that might affect an aspirant's performance, but these are not direct influences on the selection process by politicians or officers.

Summary

While no system can be entirely foolproof, the legal and operational mechanisms governing the UPSC and the CSE in India are robust and designed to minimize the influence of high-ranking officers and politicians. Although public perception may sometimes question the process, there has been no substantial evidence to suggest that the CSE selection process is systematically influenced by such external factors.

In conclusion, based on the existing framework and operational transparency, it is highly unlikely that the CSE selection process is influenced in any significant way by politicians or high-ranking officers. Nevertheless, the UPSC continues to evolve its methods to maintain and improve upon its high standards of fairness and impartiality.

HAS THE SUPREME COURT OF INDIA EVER INTERVENED IN THE CIVIL SERVICES EXAM SELECTION PROCESS? EXPLORING THE HOW, WHEN, AND POTENTIAL REASONS

The Supreme Court of India has occasionally been called upon to intervene in matters related to the Civil Services Examination (CSE) selection process conducted by the Union Public Service Commission (UPSC). However, such interventions are generally quite rare and occur in specific contexts. Below are some aspects in which the Supreme Court could or has intervened:

Legal Framework

The Supreme Court, as the apex court of India, is entrusted with upholding constitutional principles. Its role in the context of the CSE is to ensure that the examination process adheres to the principles of fairness, transparency, and equality as enshrined in the Indian Constitution.

Grounds for Intervention

1. **Discrimination or Bias**: If there are allegations of discriminatory practices in the CSE, such as those related to caste, religion, or gender, the Supreme Court may be petitioned to examine the issue.

2. **Transparency and Fairness**: The Court might intervene if there are substantial questions related to the transparency and fairness of the exam process. For instance, if the UPSC were to change the exam pattern or eligibility criteria in a way that is argued to be unfair to certain groups, it might warrant judicial review.

3. **Legal and Procedural Anomalies**: Occasionally, discrepancies in question papers, evaluation processes, or other procedural aspects may lead to legal challenges that reach the Supreme Court.

4. **Public Interest Litigations (PILs)**: PILs can be filed alleging unfair practices or demanding reforms in the CSE, which may then be examined by the Court.

Notable Instances

1. **Age Relaxation and Attempt Limit**: One notable intervention was when the Court looked into the matter of age relaxation and the number of attempts for certain categories.

2. **Reservation Policy**: The Court has been called upon to interpret and uphold the reservation policy as it applies to the CSE, balancing social justice with meritocracy.

3. **Language Issues**: The medium of examination and the option to choose regional languages have also been subjects that attracted judicial scrutiny.

Potential Reasons for Intervention

1. **Upholding Constitutional Principles**: The foremost reason is to ensure the exam process aligns with constitutional values.

2. **Addressing Public Grievances**: The Court may intervene if it believes that the UPSC's process has failed to address significant public concerns.

3. **Legal and Policy Shortcomings**: If the UPSC's existing policies have legal loopholes or are found to be lacking, the Court might step in to direct rectification.

Summary

While the UPSC enjoys considerable autonomy and is respected for its rigorous and impartial processes, the Supreme Court stands as a guardian of constitutional principles and fairness. Although its interventions in the CSE are relatively rare, they serve as important checks that add an extra layer of accountability and fairness to one of the most important examination processes in the country.

DO SELECTED CIVIL SERVANTS FACE CONFLICTS BETWEEN STATE AND CENTRAL AUTHORITIES? A COMPREHENSIVE ANALYSIS AND STRATEGIES FOR MITIGATION

Selected civil servants in India often have to navigate a complex landscape that involves both state and central authorities. The Indian administrative structure is a federal one, with clear demarcation of responsibilities between the center and the states. However, this demarcation is not always clear-cut, and overlapping jurisdictions can lead to conflicts. Here's a comprehensive analysis of some of these conflicts and strategies for their mitigation:

Types of Conflicts

1. **Jurisdictional Overlap**: Both state and central authorities may claim jurisdiction over a particular issue, leading to disputes.

2. **Resource Allocation**: Conflicts may arise when both central and state authorities lay claim to the same resources, be it financial, human, or natural.

3. **Policy Divergence**: The center and states may have different policy goals, and civil servants might find themselves caught in the middle.

4. **Political Pressures**: Different political affiliations of state and central governments can create a conflicting environment for civil servants.

5. **Administrative Procedures**: Differing norms and methods between central and state administrations can create challenges.

6. **Implementation Hurdles**: The center may design policies without adequate understanding of local conditions, leading to implementation challenges at the state level.

Strategies for Mitigation

Clarity and Communication

1. **Clear Guidelines**: Having transparent rules of engagement between central and state authorities can resolve a majority of conflicts.

2. **Regular Consultations**: Frequent dialogue between the two sides can preempt many conflicts.

Diplomacy and Tact

1. **Neutral Positioning**: Civil servants should maintain a neutral position and should not favor any party unduly.

2. **Conflict Resolution Skills**: Soft skills like negotiation and diplomacy are often as important as hard skills in mitigating conflicts.

Escalation and Legal Recourse

1. **Escalation Protocols**: A clear chain of command for escalating conflicts can lead to quick resolutions.

2. **Legal Clarity**: Understanding the constitutional provisions, laws, and statutes governing the issue at hand can help in making informed decisions.

Utilizing Technology

1. **Unified Platforms**: Creating unified platforms for data sharing and decision-making can improve transparency and reduce friction.

2. **Data-Driven Decisions**: Using data analytics to inform decisions can provide an objective basis for resolving conflicts.

Summary

While conflicts between state and central authorities are almost inevitable in a federal structure like India's, well-trained and neutral civil servants can play a critical role in mitigating these challenges. Through a mix of legal understanding, soft skills, and strategic use of technology, civil servants can ensure that the machinery of governance runs smoothly, even in a complex administrative setup.

CRAFTING THE PERFECT ESSAY FOR ACING THE CSE MAINS EXAMINATION

Writing an excellent essay is one of the most crucial parts of the Civil Services Mains Examination (CSE Mains) conducted by the Union Public Service Commission (UPSC) in India. An essay can earn you valuable marks that can be the difference between selection and missing the final list. Here's a guide on crafting the perfect essay for acing the CSE Mains:

Understanding the Format

The essay paper usually consists of two sections, each offering a choice of topics. You are required to write one essay from each section. Each essay can be between 1,000 and 1,200 words.

Choosing the Topic

1. **Area of Expertise**: Choose a subject you are comfortable with.

2. **Relevance**: The topic should ideally be current and significant.

3. **Scope for Argument**: A good essay topic allows you to present multiple perspectives.

Research and Structuring

1. **Thorough Research**: Make sure to read up on the topic from various sources.

2. **Draft an Outline**: This will be your roadmap. Break down your essay into Introduction, Body, and Conclusion.

Introduction

1. **Hook**: Start with an interesting fact or quote to grab attention.

2. **Thesis Statement**: Outline what the essay will discuss.

Body

1. **Factual Arguments**: Use data, facts, and figures to make your point.

2. **Counter-Arguments**: Mention the opposite viewpoint and refute it.

3. **Current Affairs**: Relate the topic to current events if possible.

4. **Case Studies**: Use real-life examples to make your point stronger.

Conclusion

1. **Summary**: Recap your primary points.

2. **Future Outlook**: End by discussing the future implications of your arguments.

Writing Style

1. **Formal and Impersonal**: Use the third person and keep the tone academic.

2. **Clarity over Complexity**: Simple sentences are better than complex ones if they convey the same meaning.

3. **Paragraph Transitions**: Use transition words to guide the reader.

Revision

1. **Content**: Ensure that all the points are coherent and contribute to your main argument.

2. **Grammar and Syntax**: Look out for any grammatical errors.

3. **Word Count**: Make sure you are within the prescribed word limit.

Final Tips

1. **Practice**: Write as many practice essays as you can.

2. **Feedback**: Get your essays evaluated by mentors or peers who have a good understanding of CSE Mains requirements.

3. **Time Management**: Keep track of time when you practice and during the actual exam.

By adhering to these guidelines, you can craft a compelling essay that not only meets the academic criteria but also engages the reader. So start preparing, practicing, and perfecting your essay-writing skills to ace the CSE Mains examination.

ESSENTIAL READING, TOOLS, AND STRATEGIES FOR MASTERING ESSAY WRITING IN CSE MAINS EXAMS

When it comes to preparing for the Civil Services Mains Examination (CSE Mains) conducted by India's Union Public Service Commission (UPSC), mastering essay writing can be a critical factor in your success. It's not just about showcasing your writing skills but also about presenting a well-structured argument in a limited time. Here's a roundup of essential reading materials, tools, and strategies to help you excel in this portion of the exam.

Essential Reading

1. Books

- **"A Book of Essays" by Kalpana Rajaram**: Offers a diverse set of sample essays covering various topics.

- **"151 Essays" by S.C. Gupta**: Known for its extensive list of topics and essay writing techniques.

- **"How to Write a Great Essay" by Lauren Starkey**: For general essay writing guidelines.

2. Newspapers and Journals

- **The Hindu, Indian Express**: Ideal for understanding diverse viewpoints and improving your vocabulary.

- **Economic and Political Weekly (EPW)**: Provides in-depth analysis of social and political issues.

3. Online Resources

- **UPSC Previous Years' Essay Papers**: Analyze the past papers to understand the pattern and level of complexity.

- **JSTOR, Google Scholar**: Useful for researching statistics and academic viewpoints.

Tools

1. Grammar and Spell Checkers

- **Grammarly**: For real-time grammar and style corrections.
- **Hemingway App**: To improve the readability of your essay.

2. Mind Mapping Tools

- **XMind, MindMeister**: Useful for brainstorming and organizing your thoughts.

3. Time Management Tools

- **Toggl, Be Focused**: To help you manage your time effectively while writing.

Strategies

1. PRACTICE: The 5P Strategy

- **Planning**: Allocate time for brainstorming and outlining.
- **Picking**: Choose a subject you are comfortable with.
- **Penning**: Start writing while adhering to a structured outline.
- **Proofreading**: Always spare time for revising and correcting.
- **Polishing**: Refine your essay for better coherence and flow.

2. The ICE Method

- **Idea**: Start with a central idea or thesis.
- **Citation**: Use facts, quotes, or data to support your idea.
- **Explanation**: Elaborate on how the citation proves your idea.

3. The PEEL Method

- **Point**: Make your main point in the opening sentence.
- **Evidence**: Provide evidence to support your point.
- **Explain**: Describe how this evidence supports your point.
- **Link**: Link this point to the next point or the thesis statement.

4. The Rule of Three

- **Introduction**: Clearly state what the essay will cover.

- **Body**: Limit yourself to three major points for better focus and structure.

- **Conclusion**: Sum up your main points and discuss future implications.

Armed with these readings, tools, and strategies, you'll be well-equipped to tackle the essay writing section of the CSE Mains Exam. Consistent practice and periodic review are the keys to mastering this skill.

THE SYNERGY BETWEEN PRELIMS, MAINS, AND PERSONALITY TESTS IN CSE: A DYNAMIC AND ANALYTICAL APPROACH TO UNDERSTANDING THE INTERCONNECTIONS

The Civil Services Examination (CSE) in India, one of the most challenging and prestigious examinations, is a multi-tiered process consisting of the Preliminary Exam (Prelims), the Mains Exam, and the Personality Test (Interview). Many aspirants approach these three stages as distinct, isolated challenges. However, a more effective approach lies in understanding the synergy between these components. This perspective allows for an interconnected preparation strategy, optimizing efforts and maximizing the chances of success. Let's delve deeper into how each stage correlates with the others and how to capitalize on these synergies.

The Preliminary Exam (Prelims) and Its Ripple Effect

Key Areas:

- General Studies
- Current Affairs
- Quantitative Analysis

Synergy with Mains:

- The factual information from the Prelims preparation aids in writing more accurate and data-driven answers in the Mains.
- The habit of daily newspaper reading for current affairs in Prelims can enrich your essay and General Studies answers in Mains.

Synergy with Personality Test:

- General awareness cultivated for the Prelims will make you more confident in answering current events and general knowledge questions in the Personality Test.

The Mains Exam: The Crux of CSE

Key Areas:

◆ Subjective Questions

◆ Essay Writing

◆ Optional Subjects

Synergy with Prelims:

◆ A solid understanding of general topics and current affairs from Prelims aids in the Mains.

◆ Techniques used for quick revision before the Prelims can be applied for Mains preparation.

Synergy with Personality Test:

◆ The optional subject often becomes a topic of discussion in the Personality Test.

◆ Answer writing practice for Mains can aid in articulating thoughts clearly, which is an asset in the Personality Test.

The Personality Test: More than Just an Interview

Key Areas:

◆ Communication Skills

◆ Analytical Abilities

◆ Leadership Qualities

Synergy with Prelims and Mains:

◆ Subject knowledge from Prelims and Mains makes you a more informed candidate, aiding in a more engaging discussion during the Personality Test.

◆ The confidence gained from mastering the Mains syllabus reflects in your Personality Test performance.

Strategies for a Synchronized Preparation:

1. **Integrated Note-Making:**

   Make your notes in a way that serves all three stages. Use annotations and highlights to distinguish between what is crucial for Prelims, Mains, and the Personality Test.

2. **Dynamic Study Groups:**

Being part of study groups focusing on various components of CSE can help in mutual learning and discovering links between different stages.

3. **Mock Tests and Interviews:**

Participate in tests and interviews that mimic the real examination environment. This exercise helps in understanding what to expect and how to manage time and stress, essential for all three stages.

4. **Expert Guidance:**

Seek mentorship from those who understand the interconnectedness of these stages. Their insights can save you time and effort.

By adopting a holistic view and understanding the synergies between the Prelims, Mains, and Personality Test, you can create a more streamlined, effective strategy for cracking the Civil Services Examination.

KEY SUCCESS FACTORS AND METRICS: A QUANTITATIVE GUIDE TO EFFECTIVE STRATEGIES FOR CSE ASPIRANTS

Introduction:

The Civil Services Examination (CSE), conducted by the Union Public Service Commission (UPSC) in India, is one of the most challenging competitive exams. Every year, lakhs of candidates aspire to crack this exam to secure a prestigious position in the Indian civil services. While many aspirants rely solely on qualitative approaches for preparation, this guide introduces key success factors and metrics that can be quantitatively measured, providing a data-driven methodology to enhance the effectiveness of your preparation strategies.

Core Areas Covered:

1. **Time Investment Metrics**: Optimize your study hours through data analytics.

2. **Subject-Wise Scoring Metrics**: Understand the weightage and scoring patterns of various subjects.

3. **Success Ratio Analysis**: Evaluate the success ratio for multiple-choice questions (MCQs) to inform better decision-making during the exam.

4. **Mock Test Performance Metrics**: Leverage analytics from mock tests to guide your final preparation.

Time Investment Metrics

Key Metrics:

- **Hours per Topic**: Measure the time spent on each topic.

- **Effective Study Time**: Evaluate the productivity of your study hours.

- Strategy:

- Allocate time to subjects and topics based on past years' question patterns.
- Calculate your effective study time and adjust your schedule to enhance productivity.

Subject-Wise Scoring Metrics

Key Metrics:

- **Question Frequency**: Identify the number of times a particular topic has appeared in previous exams.
- **Average Marks per Topic**: Calculate the average score you could potentially earn from each topic.

Strategy:

- Prioritize topics with higher frequency and average marks in your study plan.
- Use the metrics to decide whether to focus on breadth (covering all topics) or depth (specializing in a few high-scoring topics).

Success Ratio Analysis

Key Metrics:

- **Accuracy Rate**: Calculate the ratio of correct answers to the total number of questions attempted.
- **Risk-Reward Ratio**: Assess the ratio of marks gained to marks lost in risky questions.

Strategy:

- Aim for a higher accuracy rate in mock tests.
- Use the risk-reward ratio to decide whether or not to attempt uncertain questions during the actual exam.

Mock Test Performance Metrics

Key Metrics:

- **Score Progression**: Track your scores over multiple mock tests.
- **Time Utilization**: Measure the time taken to complete different sections of the paper.

Strategy:

◆ Use score progression to identify areas of improvement.

◆ Refine your time management skills by monitoring time utilization metrics.

Final Remarks:

Success in the CSE doesn't only depend on hard work; it also requires smart work. By understanding and applying these key success metrics, CSE aspirants can take a more informed, data-driven approach to their exam preparation, improving their chances of cracking one of the most challenging examinations in India.

COMPARING HARD WORK, SMART WORK, AND SOFT WORK FOR EFFICIENTLY ACING THE CSE EXAM

Introduction:

The Civil Services Examination (CSE) is a rigorous test of one's intellect, determination, and preparation. While hard work and discipline remain critical to success, the landscape of preparation has evolved to include smart strategies and emotional intelligence. This guide aims to provide an analytical comparison between three different approaches to preparation: Hard Work, Smart Work, and Soft Work. Each has its merits and limitations, and understanding how to blend them can significantly enhance your efficiency in acing the CSE exam.

Hard Work: The Foundation

Key Features:

◆ **Hours of Study**: Committing long hours to cover the syllabus exhaustively.

◆ **Repetition**: Regular revision to reinforce learning.

◆ **Discipline**: Strict routine and timetable.

Benefits:

◆ Mastery over subjects.

◆ Thoroughness in preparation.

◆ Resilience to face challenging questions.

Limitations:

◆ May lead to burnout.

◆ Might not be the most time-efficient method.

Smart Work: The Optimization

Key Features:

- **Selective Study**: Focusing on high-yield topics.
- **Tech Aids**: Using technology like study apps, digital notes, etc.
- **Mock Exams**: Regular self-assessment through practice exams.

Benefits:

- Time-efficient.
- Facilitates targeted learning.
- High adaptability to changing patterns of the exam.

Limitations:

- Risk of overlooking important topics.
- Dependence on external tools which may sometimes be unreliable.

Soft Work: The Emotional and Psychological Facet

Key Features:

- **Mindfulness**: Being aware of one's emotional and psychological state.
- **Stress Management**: Techniques like meditation, exercise, and short breaks to manage stress.
- **Social Skills**: Networking for knowledge sharing and moral support.

Benefits:

- Better emotional intelligence.
- Reduced exam anxiety.
- Improved focus and mental clarity.

Limitations:

- Time-consuming.
- May be considered less important and hence neglected.

Balancing the Trio for Success

1. **Blended Timetable**: Incorporate elements of all three approaches in your daily routine.

2. **Dynamic Adaptation**: Based on self-assessment, switch between the approaches as needed.

3. **Integrated Preparation Plan**: Develop a preparation plan that utilizes hard work for foundational learning, smart work for optimization, and soft work for emotional balance.

Conclusion:

While hard work lays the foundation for exam preparation, smart work adds the element of strategic optimization. Soft work, often overlooked, plays a vital role in maintaining a healthy mental and emotional state, which is crucial for optimum performance. Understanding and implementing a balanced blend of these three approaches can significantly improve your chances of acing the CSE exam.

WHAT ARE THE FACTORS THAT HINDER FOCUS, CONCENTRATION, AND DETERMINED PREPARATION FOR CSE ASPIRANTS?

Introduction:

The Civil Services Examination (CSE) demands a significant amount of focus, concentration, and determination from its aspirants. However, various factors can derail even the most committed individuals. By identifying and understanding these obstacles, aspirants can develop strategies to overcome them. Here, we delve into the primary factors that hinder focused and determined preparation for the CSE.

External Factors:

1. Digital Distractions

- **Smartphones, social media, and entertainment**: These can easily divert attention and consume a large amount of time that could be better utilized for studies.

2. Family and Social Obligations

- **Events, functions, and familial responsibilities**: These can sometimes take precedence over study time, especially in traditional societies.

3. Peer Pressure

- Comparing oneself to others can lead to demotivation or an ill-advised change in strategy.

4. Environmental Factors

- A noisy or unsuitable study environment can significantly impact concentration.

Psychological Factors:

5. Procrastination

- ◆ The tendency to postpone tasks can severely limit productivity and increase stress levels.

6. Fear and Anxiety

- ◆ Excessive worry about the outcome or the vast syllabus can paralyze efficient preparation.

7. Overwhelm

- ◆ The sheer volume of material to cover can lead to feelings of overwhelm, causing delays in starting preparation.

8. Perfectionism

- ◆ The quest for perfect notes, perfect answers, etc., can slow down the pace of preparation and lead to unnecessary stress.

Physical Factors:

9. Lack of Physical Exercise

- ◆ Physical well-being directly influences mental stamina. Lack of exercise can make one lethargic and less focused.

10. Poor Nutrition

- ◆ An inadequate diet can lead to low energy levels, making it difficult to maintain focus during long study hours.

11. Inadequate Sleep

- ◆ Lack of sleep can result in decreased mental acuity and increased stress levels.

Situational Factors:

12. Financial Constraints

- ◆ The need to work part-time or the inability to afford quality study materials can hinder preparation.

13. Lack of Guidance

♦ Not having a proper study plan or access to mentors can make the path to success more challenging.

Conclusion:

Understanding these factors can serve as the first step in overcoming them. Solutions can range from simple changes in daily habits to seeking professional guidance. Regardless, identifying these obstacles is essential for any CSE aspirant aiming for focused, concentrated, and determined preparation for this highly competitive examination.

HOW INTEGRATED SYSTEMS FOSTER NATIONAL DEVELOPMENT AND BENEFIT BOTH CSE ASPIRANTS AND SUCCESSFUL CANDIDATES

Introduction:

The integration of systems—whether it's technological, educational, or infrastructural—holds paramount importance in driving the wheels of national development. An effective, coherent system not only facilitates societal growth but also has a profound impact on individuals aiming for and working in the Civil Services. This article will explore how integrated systems contribute to national development and how they provide multiple avenues for Civil Services Examination (CSE) aspirants and successful candidates to excel in their roles as potential and actual civil servants.

For CSE Aspirants:

1. **Comprehensive Learning Platforms**
   - Integrated educational systems offer one-stop solutions for learning resources, including mock tests, current affairs updates, and more. These platforms make preparation easier and more streamlined.

2. **Skill Development Programs**
   - Integrated skill development programs offer training in soft skills, ethics, public policy, and other essential areas, preparing aspirants for the multiple facets of the civil services role.

3. **Real-Time Assessment**
   - Data analytics integrated into learning platforms can provide real-time assessment of performance, helping aspirants adapt their preparation strategies efficiently.

For Successful Candidates:

4. **E-Governance Systems**
   - A well-integrated e-governance system minimizes bureaucracy and enables efficient public service delivery, making the job of a civil servant more impactful.

5. Project Management Tools

- Integrated project management software makes it easier to oversee development projects, manage teams, and allocate resources efficiently.

6. Collaborative Frameworks

- An integrated system allows for effective interdepartmental communication and collaboration, ensuring more effective policy implementation.

For National Development:

7. Policy Formulation and Implementation

- A robust integrated system ensures that policies are well-designed and effectively implemented, thus directly contributing to national development.

8. Enhanced Public Services

- Systems integration in public services like healthcare, education, and public transport enables better resource allocation and service delivery.

9. Data-Driven Decision Making

- Integrated data analytics tools can guide policy decisions, resource allocation, and strategic development, thereby making governance more efficient and responsive to citizen needs.

Conclusion:

In a globalizing world, the integration of systems is not just an upgrade; it is a necessity for fostering national development. For CSE aspirants, these integrated systems offer a more nuanced and effective preparation route. For those who succeed in entering the civil services, they provide tools to perform their roles more effectively. Thus, as integrated systems continue to evolve, they are set to offer unprecedented opportunities for national development and for those who aim to serve their nation through the civil services.

INDIA'S CHANGE MAKERS: 100 TOP CIVIL SERVANTS AND THEIR LASTING LEGACY ON THE NATION

Compiling a list of the "top" civil servants who transformed India is subjective, and one might get different lists based on the criteria of selection. However, I can provide a list of some notable civil servants who have had a significant impact on India through their service. This list won't be exhaustive, and it might not cover 100 names due to the space constraints, but it will give a good starting point:

Name	Position	Contribution	Significance	Influence	Relevance	Impact on Today's India
V. Kurien	ICS	Father of the White Revolution	Revolutionized milk production	Dairy Development	Economic Growth	India's leadership in dairy production
T. N. Seshan	IAS (Chief Election Commissioner)	Cleaned up electoral processes	Made Election Commission a powerful body	Electoral Reforms	Democracy	Transparent election processes
S. R. Sankaran	IAS	Advocate for Dalit and tribal rights	Implemented key welfare programs	Social Welfare	Social Justice	Policies for Dalit and tribal upliftment
N. Vittal	IAS	Reforms in the telecom sector	Played a key role in telecom liberalization	Telecom Expansion	Economic Growth	Expansion of telecom services
K. J. Alphons	IAS	Demolition Man for his drive against illegal constructions	Improved urban infrastructure	Urban Development	Infrastructure	Better urban planning guidelines
Vinod Rai	IAS (CAG of India)	Exposed major scams through audit reports	Enhanced transparency and accountability	Governance	Transparency	Strengthened belief in democratic checks

Name	Position	Contribution	Significance	Influence	Relevance	Impact on Today's India
T.N. Seshan	IAS, Chief Election Commissio-ner	Transformed the Indian election system	Brought transparency, curbed electoral malpractices	Electoral Reforms	Democracy	Elevated trust in the electoral process
E. Sreedharan	IRSE (Indian Railway Service of Engineers)	Metro Man; Key role in Delhi & Kochi Metro projects	Revolutionized urban transport in India	Urban Development	Infrastructure	Catalyzed metro rail projects across India
Vinod Rai	IAS, CAG (Comptroller and Auditor General)	Unearthed major scams through audit reports	Enhanced accountability and transparency in governance	Governance	Accountability	Strengthened public faith in auditing systems
Dr. Raghuram Rajan	Economist, RBI Governor	Key economic reforms and stabilizing measures	Strengthened India's economic foundations during global financial uncertainties	Economic Policies	Financial Stability	Played a role in economic resilience during global downturns
Aruna Roy	IAS, Social Activist	Instrumental in RTI (Right to Information) Act	Democratized access to information from public authorities	Governance	Transparency	Made government workings more transparent to citizens
P.C. Parakh	IAS, Coal Secretary	Advocated for transparency in coal block allocations	Shed light on inefficiencies and potential corruption in the sector	Energy & Governance	Transparency	Pushed for reforms in the coal sector
Radhika Menon	Merchant Navy	First woman to receive the IMO Award for Exceptional Bravery at Sea	Set a benchmark for courage and duty in maritime services	Maritime Safety	Gender Equality	Recognized importance of women in maritime roles
Dr. Amrita Patel	Development professional	Chaired National Dairy Development Board	Continued the White Revolution; Dairy development	Agriculture	Food Security	Ensured growth of dairy sector post Kurien era

Name	Position	Contribution	Significance	Influence	Relevance	Impact on Today's India
R. V. Shahi	IAS, Power Secretary	Reforms in the Indian power sector	Key in electrification efforts and policy reforms	Energy	Infrastructure	Laid foundation for 24x7 power initiatives
R. K. Laxman	Cartoonist, Times of India	Political and social critiques through cartoons	Shaped public opinion, offered satirical reflections on bureaucracy	Media & Culture	Democracy	Became the voice of common man through art
V. Kurien	ICS	Father of the White Revolution	Revolutionized milk production	Dairy Development	Economic Growth	India's leadership in dairy production
T. N. Seshan	IAS (Chief Election Commissioner)	Cleaned up electoral processes	Made Election Commission a powerful body	Electoral Reforms	Democracy	Transparent election processes
S. R. Sankaran	IAS	Advocate for Dalit and tribal rights	Implemented key welfare programs	Social Welfare	Social Justice	Policies for Dalit and tribal upliftment
N. Vittal	IAS	Reforms in the telecom sector	Played a key role in telecom liberalization	Telecom Expansion	Economic Growth	Expansion of telecom services
K. J. Alphons	IAS	Drive against illegal constructions	Improved urban infrastructure	Urban Development	Infrastructure	Better urban planning guidelines
Vinod Rai	IAS (CAG of India)	Exposed major scams through audit reports	Enhanced transparency and accountability	Governance	Transparency	Strengthened belief in democratic checks
Julio Ribeiro	IPS	Anti-terrorism operations	Integral in countering terrorism in Punjab	National Security	Peace & Security	Stability in volatile regions
Kiran Bedi	IPS	Reforms in Tihar Jail	Humanized the prison system	Prison Reforms	Social Justice	Model for other prisons

Name	Position	Contribution	Significance	Influence	Relevance	Impact on Today's India
R. K. Dhowan	Naval Officer (Admiral)	Strengthening Indian Navy's operational capabilities	Led the Indian Navy during crucial times	Defense & Maritime Security	Security	Enhanced naval capabilities
Rajendra K. Pachauri	TERI	Efforts in climate change	Played a pivotal role in international climate discourse	Environment & Climate Change	Sustainability	Raised awareness about climate change
Arvind Subramanian	IAS (Chief Economic Advisor)	Economic policies & reforms	Influenced economic policymaking	Economic Development	Economic Growth	Key reforms and policies
S. Jaishankar	IFS	Diplomatic strategies	Played crucial roles in shaping India's foreign policy	Diplomacy	International Relations	Strengthened foreign relations
Durga Shakti Nagpal	IAS	Taking a strong stand against illegal sand mining	Brought focus to environmental issues and administrative integrity	Environment & Governance	Rule of Law	Inspired young aspirants and public faith in service
E. Sreedharan	IRSE (Indian Railways)	"Metro Man" - Spearheaded the Delhi Metro Rail project	Transformed urban transportation in India	Urban Transportation	Infrastructure	Made metros a reality in many Indian cities
S. Jaishankar	IFS	Played pivotal roles in India's diplomatic negotiations	Instrumental in drafting key foreign policy strategies	Diplomacy	Foreign Relations	Influenced India's global partnerships
Tuk Tuk Kumar	IFS	Work on climate change and environment diplomacy	Advocated for India's stance on climate change at global platforms	Environment Diplomacy	Sustainability	Represented India's interests in global environmental forums
Raghuram Rajan	Economist (RBI Governor)	Reforms in India's banking sector	Strengthened the financial sector and its credibility	Economic Policies	Financial Health	Ensured stability during global economic uncertainty

Name	Position	Contribution	Significance	Influence	Relevance	Impact on Today's India
Dr. W. R. Reddy	IAS	Director General of NIRDPR	Contributed significantly to rural development initiatives	Rural Development	Socio-Economic Growth	Pioneered several rural growth initiatives
B. Raman	IPS, RAW	Intelligence and security operations	Strengthened India's intelligence gathering capabilities	National Security	Security & Intelligence	Played key roles in various covert operations
Swaminathan Aiyar	Economist	Advocacy of economic liberalization	Influenced economic thought and policy-making in India	Economic Development	Policy Making	Instrumental in shaping liberal economic policies
Dr. Amrita Patel	NDDB Chairman	Continued the White Revolution post Kurien	Strengthened the dairy cooperative movement	Dairy Development	Livelihoods	Ensured India's sustained growth in dairy production
Jockin Arputham	Social Worker	Advocacy for slum dwellers' rights	Brought global attention to India's urban housing issues	Urban Development	Human Rights	Pushed for inclusive urban policies
Dr. Shanta	Medical Service	Pioneer in cancer care in India	Elevated the standards of cancer treatment & research	Healthcare	Public Health	Helped establish leading cancer care institutes
P. S. Appu	IAS	Reforms in the administration of tribal and rural areas	Brought transparency and focus to rural development	Rural Development	Governance	Set standards for equitable rural governance
N. Gopalaswami	IAS (Chief Election Commissioner)	Electoral reforms and introducing EVMs	Digitalized and streamlined the election process in India	Electoral Reforms	Democracy	Elevated the trust in electronic voting
Tessy Thomas	DRDO Scientist	"Missile Woman" of India	Instrumental in the development of Agni series of ballistic missiles	Defense & Technology	National Security	Strengthened India's missile defense system

Name	Position	Contribution	Significance	Influence	Relevance	Impact on Today's India
Raju Narayana Swamy	IAS	Reforms in agricultural productivity & administration	Focused on transparent and efficient agricultural practices	Agriculture	Economic Growth	Pioneered various agro-based initiatives
U. Sagayam	IAS	Notable anti-corruption initiatives	Set a benchmark for integrity in civil services	Governance	Transparency	Became a symbol of incorruptible governance
Sam Pitroda	Technocrat	Led India's telecommunication revolution	Pivotal in democratizing telecommunication access	Telecom & Innovation	Economic Growth	Laid foundation for India's IT boom
Montek Singh Ahluwalia	Economist (Deputy Chairman, Planning Commission)	Architect of economic liberalization	Key in shaping India's economic reforms in the early '90s	Economic Policies	Economic Development	Steered significant economic policies
Harish Hande	Social Entrepreneur	Promoting sustainable energy solutions	Spearheaded grassroots-level sustainable energy initiatives	Sustainable Energy	Environmental Sustainability	Propagated the importance of renewable energy
K. J. Alphons	IAS	Known as "Demolition Man" for his drive against illegal constructions	Brought focus on urban planning and governance	Urban Development	Governance	Advocacy for planned urban development
R. S. Sharma	IAS	Instrumental in Aadhaar project and telecom reforms	Played key roles in digital identity and telecom sectors	Digital India & Telecom	Governance	Pushed for digitization and reforms in telecom
V. Shunglu	IAS	Led several high-profile audit investigations	Brought transparency and integrity in administrative audits	Governance	Accountability	Ensured accountability in public projects
Kiran Bedi	IPS	First woman officer in IPS, significant reforms in Tihar Jail	Advocated for prison reform and women's empowerment in police	Law & Order	Gender Equality	Set standards for policing and reforms

Name	Position	Contribution	Significance	Influence	Relevance	Impact on Today's India
Ajit Doval	IPS, Intelligence	Played key roles in various intelligence and diplomatic missions	Strengthened India's internal and external security	National Security	Diplomacy	Significant contributions in strategic defense
Bimal Jalan	Economist (RBI Governor)	Banking and economic reforms during his tenure at RBI	Guided Indian economy during crucial periods	Economic Policies	Financial Health	Managed economy during Asian financial crisis
S.R. Shankaran	IAS	Advocacy for rights of Scheduled Castes and Scheduled Tribes	Pioneered social justice initiatives	Social Welfare	Inclusion	Championed the rights of marginalized communities
Anil Swarup	IAS	Reforms in Coal Sector and Education	Streamlined coal block allocations & pushed for education reforms	Energy & Education	Governance	Played pivotal roles in policy formulation
Rajni Razdan	IAS	Served in UPSC, known for administrative reforms	Brought greater transparency in recruitment processes	Governance	Recruitment	Streamlined UPSC's functioning and processes
Dr. M. S. Swaminathan	Agricultural Scientist	"Father of Green Revolution" in India	Revolutionized Indian agriculture	Agriculture	Food Security	Led the transformation of Indian agriculture